Design
Through
Discovery
The Elements
and Principles

Hillary T. Chisholm

Design Through Discovery

The Elements and Principles

Marjorie Elliott Bevlin

Holt Rinehart Winston

New York   Chicago   San Francisco
Philadelphia   Montreal   Toronto   London
Sydney   Tokyo   Mexico City   Rio de Janeiro   Madrid

Publisher: Susan Katz
Acquiring Editor: Karen Dubno
Project Editor: Lisa Owens
Copy Editor: Lauren Root
Picture Editor: Joan Scafarello
Picture Research: Marion Geisinger
Permissions Editor: Nicolette C. Harlan
Production Manager: Nancy Myers
Composition and camera work: York Graphic Services
Color separations: The Lehigh Press, Inc.
Printing and binding: R. R. Donnelley & Sons Co.

Reproduced on the cover:
Miriam Schapiro, *Mexican Memory*. 1981.
Acrylic, fabric, and glitter on canvas.
4 × 8′ (1.22 × 2.44 m)
Collection of Lynne and Jeffrey Slutsky.
Courtesy Barbara Gladstone Gallery.

Library of Congress Cataloging in Publication Data

Bevlin, Marjorie Elliott.
   Design through discovery—the elements and principles.

   Constitutes the first 10 chapters of the 4th ed. of
the author's *Design Through Discovery*.
   Bibliography: p. 165
   Includes index.
   1. Design.   I. Bevlin, Marjorie Elliott.   Design
Through Discovery.   II. Title.
NK1510.B532   1985   745.4   84-6617

ISBN 0-03-071624-1

5 6 7 8   039   9 8 7 6 5 4 3 2

CBS COLLEGE PUBLISHING

Holt, Rinehart and Winston
The Dryden Press
Saunders College Publishing

TO RUSS
who might have used it.

Preface

During the twenty years in which DESIGN THROUGH DISCOVERY has been used as a design textbook, many teachers have expressed a need for a briefer version that would present the elements and principles of two- and three-dimensional design without the subsequent chapters on the various fields of application. Such a text would be relatively inexpensive and would be more directly suited to the limited content of beginning design courses. This edition is offered in response to that need.

DESIGN THROUGH DISCOVERY: THE ELEMENTS AND PRINCIPLES is, in fact, the first ten chapters of the fourth edition of DESIGN THROUGH DISCOVERY. Chapters 1 and 2 give an overview showing that design is not only a discipline to be studied but the underlying order of the universe. We *discover* this order by our awareness, seeing texture in a geological formation, discerning lines in bare trees, recognizing rhythm through our heartbeat and the seasons. Just as design determines our biological lives, so we become designers by controlling our personal environment. By enlightened selection as well as by craftsmanship, we create our surroundings, choosing the colors, textures, and types of furnishings that give us a sense of home and well-being.

The elements—line, shape, mass, space, texture, and color—are described and explained in Chapters 3 through 7. The principles—unity, variety, balance, emphasis, rhythm, proportion, and scale—are discussed and their meaning illustrated in Chapters 8 through 10. A wealth of visual illustration from all of the design disciplines is used, in the interest of clarity and to emphasize the richness of design reflected in and fundamental to all areas of human life. There are 208 black-and-white illustrations and 22 color plates in all. Of particular importance is the complete design bibliography, referring not only to the ten chapters of this edition but to all facets of the field of design.

Most important of all perhaps, DESIGN THROUGH DISCOVERY: THE ELEMENTS AND PRINCIPLES seeks to establish that design is a source of truth. Through the centuries, in a world often harsh and chaotic, the elements and principles of design have remained unchanged. The cave drawings of 12,000 B.C. exhibit the same rhythm and linear quality that are essential to the design of the newest skyscraper. We have selected illustrations that demonstrate this timelessness, with the goal of providing the student with the secure knowledge that design in all its manifestations is, indeed, eternal. This knowledge can become the cornerstone both for an artist's career and for a philosophy of living in an ever-changing world.

Acknowledgments

I have been given immeasurable help by a diversified group of professors who have taken the time and painstaking effort to assess the manuscript in detail, in the light of their own students' needs. It would be impossible to express how much the present edition is indebted to their perceptive comments and suggestions. My sincere appreciation goes to Timothy T. Blade, University of Minnesota, Twin Cities; Mel Casas, San Antonio College, Texas; William Holley, East Carolina University, North Carolina; Jo A. Lonam, California State University, Sacramento; Lon Nuell, Middle Tennessee State University, Murfreesboro; Harper T. Phillips, Bergen Community College, New Jersey; Carol S. Robertson, Bauder Fashion College, Georgia; Rick Rodrigues, City College of San Francisco; Patricia Terry, The University of Southwestern Louisiana; Mary VanRoekel, North Dakota State University, Fargo; Nicholas H. von Bujdoss, Smith College, Massachusetts; and Lee Wright, The University of Texas, Arlington.

I am indebted as well to Dr. Donald R. Woods of McMaster University for his suggestions in the area of problem solving.

My very special thanks go to Karen Dubno, Art Editor, and Lisa Owens, Project Editor, at Holt, Rinehart and Winston, who directed the production of the book from start to finish, providing guidance while still allowing me to make the book my own, a feat requiring a rare combination of tact, understanding, and editorial skill. I am also much indebted to Joan Scafarello, who was in charge of obtaining illustrations, and to Marion Geisinger, who spent long hours at the task, a tedious and frequently frustrating undertaking.

Finally, my appreciation goes, as always, to my family for their support and interest, and to the many friends who bore with me throughout my preoccupation, several of whom contributed helpful research material. Among these last, I would especially mention Michael Boyd and Gladys and Al Walker.

M.E.B.

Cragbourne
Orcas Island, Washington
September 1984

Contents

10 Proportion and Scale 144

Proportion   *The Golden Mean*   *The Fibonacci Series*   Scale

Glossary   159
Bibliography   165
Index   169
Photographic Credits   171

xi *Contents*

Design
Through
Discovery
The Elements
and Principles

The Essence of Design

Design is the organization of parts into a coherent whole. Although it is considered to be a human expression, design is in reality the underlying process by which the universe was formed through orderly procedures of selection and evolution. The resulting phenomena often reveal a perfection far beyond the capabilities of human designers, yet they have the potential to offer limitless inspiration (Fig. 1).

The incredibly complex design of our universe continues to baffle scientists. No choreographer could plot a network of movements as intricate as the revolution of moons around planets, planets around their stars, stars whirling in their galaxies, and galaxies interrelated in a system whose limits we have only begun to explore. On our own Earth—a small planet belonging to a small star, the Sun—we can identify a complicated design of water and land, mountains and deserts, forests and plains. What through the centuries has been erected over this topography seems to be the creation solely of human designers—a superficial pattern laid upon the surface of the land. Actually these human constructions, farms, cities, and nations, were determined largely by the natural design that existed before them. Areas of fertility yield patches of growth (Fig. 2); rivers and natural harbors form obvious sites for the construction of cities; and mountain ranges, rivers, and other bodies of water mark the boundaries between nations. In contrast, deserts, towering mountains, and dense jungles retain their primal character by defying the possibility of any human imprint. Even the seacoasts, pounded by surf, retain a stark beauty, having triumphed over human invasion. The repetition of natural forms in eroded rock and ebbing

1
Victor B. Scheffer. Green sea anemone,
Anthopleura xanthogrammica, Olympic seacoast,
Washington. Photograph.

2
Aerial photo of terraced farms in central Peru.

3

4

tide creates a continually changing masterpiece of design (Fig. 3). Taken in its totality then, our environment, both constructed and natural, can be considered the actual character of the earth, the result of the natural forces inherent in its composition.

Other designs of astonishing complexity appear in the food chains of animals and fish and in the interdependence of insects and plants (Fig. 4). The mechanisms of organisms are functional designs of a high order. Most sophisticated of all is the human body, with its neurological, muscular, circulatory, digestive, eliminative, and reproductive functions all evolved to a high degree.

With such order underlying every aspect of our universe, it is not surprising that the desire for order should have become a basic human characteristic. In every culture, every mythology, and every religion, the world began when order was created out of chaos. The book of Genesis, the foundation stone of the Judeo-Christian tradition, reads like a classic design scheme (Fig. 5). Greek mythology is founded upon a process in which the entire complicated genealogy of the gods can be traced back to the ancestors who sprang from chaos and then sorted the universe into categories, giving Zeus dominion over the land, Poseidon over the seas, and Hades over the underworld. Further subdivisions allocated the Dawn, the Harvest, the Hunt, Love, and so forth. Both the ancient Chinese and the ancient Egyptians believed in a nebulous state that existed before the earth came into being. In all these versions the world as we know it began only when confusion or nothingness gave way to form and order—in other words, to design.

The great religions of the world have carried design further, into the systems of ethics by which people can live in harmony with one another and the universe. The Hebrew Torah, the writings of Confucius and Lao-Tse, the Hindu Vedas, the New Testament, and the Muslim Koran are all bodies of instruction seeking to create order in both individual and collective human lives.

3
Victor B. Scheffer. *Surf at South Point, Island of Hawaii.* Photograph.

4
David Cavagnaro. *Orb Weaver Spider Web.* 1970. Photograph.

5
The Creation of the World. 13th century. Vault mosaic. St. Mark's Cathedral, Venice.

6
Moraine Lake, near Banff, Alberta, Canada.

The quest for order did not stop with the arrangement of philosophical priorities, however. It continued in the establishment of nations, the formation of medieval guilds, and the design of planned communities. Today the process gives rise to such diversified groups as the proponents of Esperanto (the international language), the European Common Market, the Arab League, and the Women's Movement, all designed to sort out areas of increasing importance and to place them in an orderly context with existing practices and organizations.

In nature, the endless cycle of birth, death, and renewal can result in what appears to be a chaotic tangle . Taming the wilderness, the traditional beginning for pioneers moving onto a new frontier, meant the ordering of such chaos for human use. Today, in a world threatened with overpopulation and destructive technology, we see the wilderness rather as a treasure to be protected. This idea inspired one of the most vital and sensitive of designs, the creation of national parks and wilderness areas. In all parts of the earth, regions of particular scenic or ecological interest have now been set aside for preservation, scientific study, and human enjoyment. In Italy, India, and Africa national parks provide protection for animals, from the chamois to the Asian lion, while the first national park in the United States was established to protect the geysers, hot springs, and other phenomena unique to the Yellowstone region of Wyoming. All such parks are carefully designed to maintain a delicate balance between human enjoyment and ecological preservation. Roads are unobtrusive, and inns, lodges, shops, and cabin accommodations are designed in rustic styles that blend with the natural surroundings. Miles of trails lead to lakes and mountain tops and strategically located campsites make an extended visit possible. While the emphasis is placed on the preservation of natural beauty and wildlife, human needs are served in a variety of ways (Fig. 6).

5

6

Increased emphasis on human needs is obvious in the design of model cities, apartment complexes, and shopping malls. The World Trade Center in Dallas (Fig. 7) is the last in a six-building complex comprising the Dallas Market Center, a 125-acre (50-hectare) beehive of trade shops. In planning the World Trade Center, the builders wished to erect a structure that would be usable year-round, even in Dallas' hot climate; that would provide for easy passage within the building and to the others in the complex; that would categorize certain types of shops; and, finally, that would give the feeling of a town square.

Architects Beran and Shelmire solved all these problems with a soaring, open-core structure of seven floors (eventually to be twenty). Since the entire facility is enclosed, climate can be regulated to a comfortable springlike atmosphere. All the shops open from balconies located mostly around the central courtyard. The various floors are connected by high-speed escalators and glass-enclosed elevators, while carpeted halls lead to the other buildings. Each level has been assigned to an individual type of shop, with gifts on the second floor, fabrics on the third, and so forth. Best of all, the core of the building succeeds beautifully at creating the effect of a pleasant city plaza. The floor is cobbled, trees and plants abound, a central pool-fountain provides a gathering point for people, and the whole is lighted by an immense natural skylight. In all respects, the World Trade Center has been pronounced a resounding success.

We have mentioned designs that involve economic considerations, moral values, and philosophical beliefs. In the last two examples discussed, national parks and the World Trade Center, function and visual pleasure are inseparable. This is not unusual. Most designs that function well are visually satisfying. A town that has grown up serving the needs of its inhabitants usually presents an orderly and attractive appearance (Fig. 8). A book, a pot, a skyscraper, or a stage set that is functionally successful will almost certainly be satisfying to the eye as well.

In visual design, satisfying the eye is an important aspect of function. The effectiveness of any work of art lies in certain elements and principles that govern its creation and in the impact these have on our senses and emotions. This is true of the work of the writer and musical composer as well as of the work of the visual artist. To put it simply, music enters the consciousness through the sense of hearing, from which point it can involve our emotions, often affecting us deeply. We can be just as deeply affected by experiences that enter our consciousness through the sense of sight. Visual experiences can arouse our curiosity or simply inform us. It is with these visual experiences that we are primarily concerned.

The Psychology of Seeing

Fundamental to either creating or appreciating a visual design is the process of *seeing*. Sensations enter the human eye through the *lens,* a flattened sphere constructed of numerous transparent fibers, which flattens or becomes more spherical depending upon its distance from the object to be viewed. The lens brings images of such objects to the light-sensitive *retina* where the images are registered; in fact, the retina of an eye removed from either a human being or an animal will frequently show a complete image of the world toward which the eye had been turned.

What happens after the image reaches the retina has long been a subject

7
Beran and Shelmire. Hall of Nations in the World Trade Center, Dallas Market Center, Texas. Completed 1974.

8
Aerial view of San Gimignano, Italy, a medieval town.

of philosophical and psychological debate. The ancient Greeks tended to stress the unreliability of the senses generally, since individuals react differently to sounds and tastes and see shapes and colors differently. The realization that a stick dipped in water looked broken and the edges of a road seemed to meet in the distance when they knew this was not true only reinforced their distrust of the human eye. As a result, one of the functions of the intellect was assumed to be the correction of the senses in order to establish the truth. Reason was called upon to be the guide in evaluating perception.

Later thinkers, including Leonardo da Vinci, felt that the eye had power to extend rays to the object viewed as well as to take in images emanating from it. Contemporary thought might conceivably be considered a philosophical extension of this theory, for experiments have proven that perception is not a simple, purely sensory mirroring but a process involving selective acts of considerable intricacy. The word *Gestalt,* which translates from the German as "form," is used to describe the fact that we tend to seize our visual experiences as total unified configurations. This is achieved through a sequence of phases in which our individual brains perform the act of *closure,* unifying our perceptions into an order in which our intelligence, memory, and visual perceptions are refined to acknowledge a specific shape, size, or color. We see four lines and perceive that they are a square because by the act of closure we have imposed our own order upon them. Color, too, is perceived through a series of reactions to the light that is admitted to the brain as electromagnetic energy (see Chapter 7).

Studies have shown that the act of seeing is influenced not only by the viewer's intelligence and memory but by race, cultural group, and amount

7

8

9

of training. Seeing, therefore, becomes a personal experience conditioned by thought processes, memory, and associations, leading to widely differing interpretations of any given subject (p. 15).

With this brief consideration of what is involved in the process of seeing, we will now explore the characteristics of visual design.

Definition of Visual Design

In order to understand what we mean by a visual design, we must first make a distinction between art and design. *Art is concerned with the creation of a work that will arouse an aesthetic response.* "Aesthetic" derives from the Greek *aisthetikos,* pertaining to sense perception, and although for centuries this meant that art was expected to be beautiful, today we extend the range of response to include the entire gamut of human reaction. What we perceive with our eyes—in paintings, sculpture, drawings, prints, and photographs—may result in our feeling delight, admiration, shock, rapture, intrigue, disquiet, revulsion, or even disinterest. The important point is that the aesthetic experience is the work's primary purpose. The artist also undergoes an aesthetic experience in creating the work. In this context, art is a form of communication: the artist expresses and the viewer responds. To carry the definition a step further, it could be said that art rises above the utilitarian aspects of everyday living to spiritual levels.

A design has an explicit purpose. We have already discussed the broad application of the term *design* in the world of nature and human relationships, noting reasons for designs in these areas. A visual design has many possible reasons for being, or *purposes,* ranging from household efficiency to the encouragement of self-esteem. In the pages that follow we will discover a fascinating range of such possibilities.

It is of the utmost importance that we understand that art and design, while representing two distinct fields of activity, are in their fundamental aspects closely related. A work of art depends upon a framework of design in order to achieve its aesthetic character. A design, in turn, may have a strong aesthetic quality. In their own distinctive ways, both a motorcycle and a painting can be beautiful.

9
Piet Mondrian's studio in New York, 1940s.
10
Piet Mondrian.
Composition with Red, Yellow, and Blue.
1939–42. Oil on canvas, 28⅝ × 27¼"
(72.4 × 69.2 cm). Tate Gallery, London.

This relationship is not accidental. It is the result of a body of specific elements and principles governing the creation of both works. The elements—line, shape and mass, space, texture, and color—are the ingredients with which the artist or designer works. The principles—unity and variety, balance, emphasis, rhythm, proportion, and scale—provide the means by which the elements can be combined in an aesthetic way. The purpose of this book is to show how these elements and principles operate, not only in design but in the field of art, and to illustrate the basic importance of these elements and principles in all creative activity.

In visual terms, design is the *organization* of *materials* and *forms* in such a way as to fulfill a specific *purpose*. There are four ideas here: organization or order, materials, form, and purpose. Although they are interwoven in the creation of any effective design, we will discuss each one separately.

A Plan for Order

Throughout the height of his career, the Dutch artist Piet Mondrian created paintings that consist of precise squares and rectangles in black, white, and the primary colors (red, yellow, and blue). It would be difficult to find more ordered works of art than these. Although Mondrian's sense of organization carried him to extremes of method, we can learn much about the way an artist organizes a composition by studying his working habits.

Figure 9 shows Mondrian's studio in New York, where he moved toward the end of his life. On the walls are fixed rectangles in different sizes of black, white, and colors. According to his biographers, it was the artist's custom to arrange and rearrange these rectangles on the wall constantly until he had arrived at a pattern that satisfied him. Similar relationships can be found in his precise, geometric paintings (Fig. 10).

Many times artists follow this procedure to plot out a design, working perhaps with scraps of paper or pieces of fabric. Preliminary drawings for a painting or sculpture do the same job, as do architects' sketches and scale models. All of these are plans for order—the first step in creative design.

10

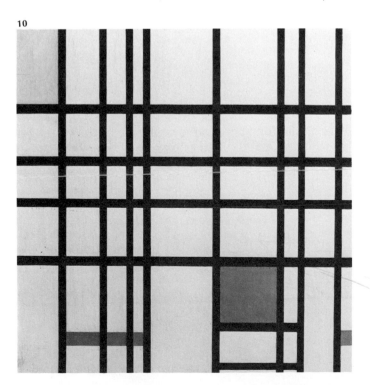

11

11
Auguste Rodin. *The Danäid.* 1885. Marble,
13¾ × 28½ × 22½" (34.9 × 72.4 × 57.2 cm).
Rodin Museum, Paris.

12
Auguste Rodin. *Monument to Balzac.*
1897–98. Bronze (cast 1954), height 8'10"
(2.69 m), at base 48¼ × 41" (1.23 × 1.04 m).
Museum of Modern Art, New York (presented
in memory of Curt Valentin by his friends).

13
Michelangelo. *David.* 1501–04.
Marble, height 18' (5.48 m).
Academy, Florence.

14
David Smith. *Zig IV.* 1961.
Steel, painted yellow-gold;
7'9⅜ × 7¼ × 6'4"
(2.37 × 2.14 × 1.93 m).
Vivian Beaumont Theater, Lincoln Center
for the Performing Arts, New York
(purchased with funds contributed
by Howard and Jean Lipman).

Expression of Materials

Much of the impact of a design will depend upon the way the artist uses particular materials. Oil paints can be laid on in transparent glazes, or they can be applied with a palette knife in a thick plastic buildup known as *impasto.* Wood can be finished until it is almost as smooth as glass, or left rough, in the manner of driftwood.

The two sculptures shown in Figures 11 and 12 are the work of a single artist, Auguste Rodin. The strikingly different treatment of forms, surface, and modeling can be attributed at least in part to Rodin's feelings about two different materials—marble and bronze. In the marble *Danaïd* (Fig. 11) we see a smoothly polished, luminous interpretation of the nude. Every bone, every muscle, is beautifully expressed, and the figure's flesh almost seems as though it would be warm to the touch. Rodin clearly was responding to the pure sensuousness of the marble in designing this work. The bronze *Balzac* (Fig. 12) is quite another matter. Here the artist wished to create an impression of overwhelming monumentality, of sheer power, in the personality of the French writer. Physical characteristics yield to the dynamic flow of Balzac's cloak, a movement culminating in a head whose features are highly stylized. The character's essential dynamism is depicted through the inherent strength and force of the bronze itself.

Some artists construct forms specifically to exploit the characteristics of a chosen material. Michelangelo loved the beauty of the marble in the hills of his native Italy, and he used it for his sculpture whenever possible. He blocked out the stone while it was still in the quarry, directing the workmen to cut pieces in which he saw particular beauty. When asked how he had carved the magnificent *David* (Fig. 13), he replied that he had simply chiseled away the stone until the figure was liberated. To him, the stone was a living entity and each block unique, with a form waiting inside to be released.

In the years following World War II, several sculptors became intrigued

by the possibilities of metal. These artists saw welding techniques as a means to tremendous freedom of expression, and they began to experiment with forms that were cut from sheets of steel and other metals. Within a few years the entire concept of sculpture had been altered (Fig. 14).

Designers approach their work in different ways. Some *plan* a specific object with its purpose in mind, and all other considerations are secondary. Many designers, however, visualize first in terms of form. They have an idea, and they choose a medium in which to express it, just as a sculptor who creates a portrait bust has a choice of working in bronze, stone, plaster, clay, acrylic, wood, or even fiber. The selection of the material is a major decision in terms of how it will best realize the specific form.

Form

The world around us is composed of *physical* forms, from the pebble that can be held in the hand to the mountain that requires days to climb. Trees that at a distance are flatly silhouetted against the horizon become at close range three-dimensional forms that can be walked around and viewed from all sides. Form, however, is not a synonym for mass or volume. A two-dimensional object can have form just as a three-dimensional one does. When shape is governed by structural considerations, it becomes form. In other words, the silhouetted tree is still a form because its shape is determined by the structure of the tree. It is only our perception and the conditions governing it that transform the tree into a flat shape. A round shadow on a wall is a shape, but the street sign casting the shadow is a form. Form, then, is the shape and structure of an object.

12
13

14

The term *form* may also refer to medium or subject matter in a work of art. A sculptor's work may be in the form of stone; a painter's canvases may be in the form of landscapes. There are other uses of the term, for instance, form as the physical being of an object (the female form) or as its physical composition (a solid or a vaporous form).

From the standpoint of the designer, form is the particular combination of sizes, shapes, and masses that compose a work and cause that work to exist in the space around it. The artist organizes these elements into an integrated entity. As the artist works with the elements and principles of design, form emerges, a material embodiment of the message of the senses and emotions.

Form can spring entirely from the artist's imagination (Fig. 15) or it can be controlled to some extent by tradition. Christian tradition, for instance, requires that a church be adorned in some way with a cross. The Mohammedan religion forbids the use of the human figure, so Islamic art is rich in geometric and abstract forms.

Form is dictated by the purpose a designed object must serve. A chair must have a horizontal plane for sitting, a cup must be hollow to contain liquids, a bracelet must fit an arm or ankle. These considerations bring us to the fourth concern in our definition of visual design.

15

15
Joan Miró. *Self-Portrait I.* 1937–38. Pencil, crayon, and oil on canvas; 4'9½" × 3'2¼" (1.46 × .97 m). Museum of Modern Art, New York. James Thrall Soby Bequest.

16
Blickensderfer electric typewriter. 1902. Courtesy British Typewriter Museum, Bournemouth, England.

17
Olivetti ET 225 electronic typewriter.

18
Totem pole, Stanley Park, Vancouver, B.C.

16
17

18

Fulfillment of Purpose

Although intuition and other personal qualities play a large part in the design process, concern for the purpose of the design must be the first priority of any designer. In utilitarian objects—home furnishings, utensils, clothing—this purpose is clear, yet there are many ways in which a design problem can be handled. The diversity of possibilities can be seen in the two typewriters shown in Figures 16 and 17. Both are electric, designed for the same purpose, yet the span of three-quarters of a century separating the designs has resulted in dramatic refinements in the concept of how a type-writer should look. In creating the 1902 model, the designer was obviously concentrating on the utilitarian aspects of an invention that was less than thirty years old. Seventy-five years later, the designer could take function more or less for granted, freeing the attention to consider such elements as proportion, color, line, and texture. This in no way implies that the later machine is a better design; the modern typewriter simply incorporates more varied considerations.

Some works serve purposes on several levels. The totem poles carved by the Indians of the Pacific Northwest (Fig. 18) are strong in design qual-ity, yet they have as their purpose the keeping of tribal records. Stylized characters representing the Indians' animal companions of land and sea and air are carved in exciting variety into the huge pole of Northwest cedar, adding visual drama and meaning to the depiction of the clan's

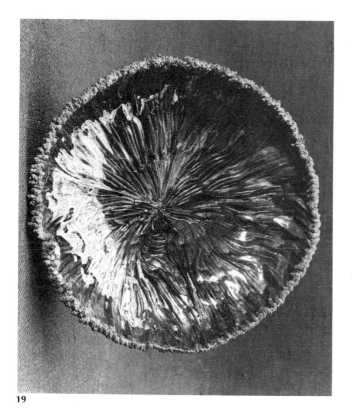

19

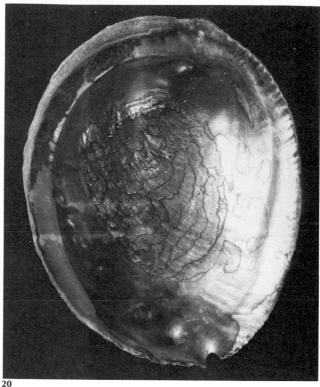

20

history. Remaining visible under the sculpture and paint, the majestic tree narrates the personal and familial legend of the chief of the clan and records the social and religious philosophy of a people. Even to the casual viewer, however, the totem pole is a work of striking design. Appreciation of this fact operates independently of any knowledge of Indian symbolism.

The Role of the Designer

The designer brings two important ingredients to any creative work: *inspiration,* which gives birth to a particular design, and *originality,* which sets it apart from other designs.

Inspiration

The creative designer observes the universe with sensitivity, absorbing impressions from all around. These impressions drop into the subconscious mind like cells that divide and combine to form new entities, which could never be constructed by conscious effort. Often when one least expects it, one becomes aware of new relationships and, seeing them in unique terms, works to give them a form that will make them apparent to others. This, in essence, is the phenomenon known as *inspiration.*

Looking at June Schwarcz' enamel bowl in Figure 19, we can see a striking resemblance to the haliotis shell (Fig. 20). The roughness of the exterior and the iridescent quality of the inside of the bowl are both strongly reminiscent of the shell. The fluted appearance of the interior of

19
June Schwarcz. Electroformed enamel bowl 571. 1970. Copper enamel; diameter 11″ (28 cm), height 2¾″ (7 cm). Courtesy Mrs. K. Reichert, San Diego, Calif.

20
Haliotis fulgens,
a shell found on the beaches of California.

21
Clitocybe dealbata, subspecies *sudorifica.* Toadstools.

12   *Design Through Discovery*

the bowl is strikingly like a toadstool (Fig. 21) or like other forms of sea life (Fig. 177, p. 135). The artist had no intention of *imitating* any of these objects, but in delving into her personal experience she, consciously or unconsciously, combined characteristics of two things she had found interesting. Her reactions to these natural forms and her ability to see their characteristics in a totally new relationship provided the inspiration for her bowl.

Since inspiration is nourished by impressions, it becomes imperative that the artist absorb through the senses as much of the world as possible. One designer may find motivation in travel to other lands, another in films of space flight, yet another in the sight of a familiar weed. Some artists draw their ideas directly from their own memories and experiences. Generally speaking, the more one is exposed to sights, sounds, smells, and textures, the more one learns of the arts of theater, dance, poetry, and music; and to the extent one attempts to understand the workings of science and technology, one is likely to arrive at designs that will awaken response in a variety of people.

The New Mexico-based artist Georgia O'Keeffe has executed a series of paintings based on flowers (Pl. 1, p. 19). Her particular approach causes her to move in very close on the subject, so that the flowers open up and expand to create a whole universe. Seeing these natural forms through O'Keeffe's eyes, we become aware of them as shapes and patterns as well as living personalities. Inspiration was derived from a delicate botanical specimen, but the artist's unique viewpoint gave this sensitive expression of beauty a feeling of monumentality.

Originality

Originality of design results from individuality in the designer. Today there is increased emphasis on individuality in reaction to computerized civilization and worldwide standardization. Ease of transportation has brought widely separated cultures together, made possible instant communication, and caused formerly isolated cultures to be invaded and in some cases destroyed. In a world where it is possible to eat hamburgers in Tokyo and sukiyaki in New York, the potential for uniqueness in a human being is not something to be taken for granted.

21

22

In former generations of children, the first five highly impressionable years could be filled with a wealth of personal exploration, uninhibited fantasy, and rich associations derived from family experiences and imaginative reactions to stories. The advent of television, however, has bombarded the child with a conformity of influences almost as soon as that child learns to focus. Thus, kindergarten classmates have a store of reference material in common with children all over the nation, if not the world. Since characters, settings, and other data are presented on television with all details visually complete, the imaginative efforts of children are not called upon to create but must be exercised in the adaptation and expansion of things already seen. Fortunately, imagination is a strong trait in most children, and in spite of this narrowing band of experience their imagination will express itself in daydreaming and play.

Imagery *translating a personal image*

The Dutch artist M. C. Escher (Fig. 22) describes his work as an effort to communicate ideas springing from his amazement and wonder at the laws of nature that operate in the world around us. Although his works involve a wide variety of subjects and forms, any one of them immediately proclaims itself as the creation of this particular artist, for it is the result of a highly personal *imagery* expressed in personal stylization.

Imagery lies behind any work of art, for it is in translating a personal image that the artist achieves artistic expression. In another sense, imagery can be defined as the *act* of making images, as in drawing or painting. Images can be direct representations of people, places and things, but they can also become *symbols,* evoking other things and ideas. The concept of imagery may become clearer when we contrast two types: *perceptual* and *conceptual.*

Perceptual Imagery

Perception relates to *real things* that actually exist or that actually did exist and survive in memory. No two people perceive in exactly the same way,

22
M. C. Escher.
Concave and Convex. 1955.
Lithograph, 10⅞ × 13⅛"
(27.5 × 33.5 cm).
Haagsgemeentemuseum, The Hague.
23
John Marin.
Woolworth Building, New York, No. 3.
1913. Etching, 12⅞ × 10½"
(33.02 × 26.6 cm). Brooklyn
Museum (Dick S. Ramsay Fund).
24
Joseph Stella. *Skyscrapers.*
1922. Mixed media on canvas,
8'3¾ × 4'6" (2.53 × 1.37 m).
Newark Museum, New Jersey.

as we noted in discussing the psychology of seeing (p. 6). Even artists who strive for realistic representation of what they see will necessarily be influenced by a personal perception.

We can understand this by looking at two remarkably different interpretations of the New York City skyline. Neither artist in this case was striving for realistic representation, yet perception was the starting point for both interpretations.

John Marin, an early twentieth-century American watercolorist, was especially sensitive to atmospheric effects. In his etching of the *Woolworth Building* (Fig. 23) this sensitivity is translated into the image of a skyscraper being tossed about by the wind. Millions of people have seen the Woolworth Building from the exact spot where Marin stood, and many on just such a windy day. However, it was Marin's special *perception* of the scene that led to this particular *imagery*.

A more conventional attitude toward skyscrapers, though not necessarily a conventional image, appears in Joseph Stella's painting (Fig. 24). Here the image is one of strict geometry, soaring verticality, buildings reaching up to the skies. Stella's skyscrapers would never bend before the wind. They are instead closely spaced spires, almost like the spires on a cathedral, perhaps signaling the new religion of technology. Again, the artist builds his imagery from his own perceptions of a subject.

23

24

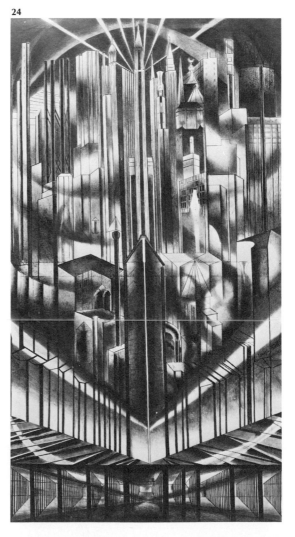

Conceptual Imagery

A conceptual image is a kind of symbol, a shape or form that represents something in the artist's mind rather than what is actually seen. In other words, it is the artist's personal concept of a subject. Conceptual imagery derives from emotion, fantasy, or invention.

One thinks of the eye as being like a camera, but the human eye does not actually record complete and separate pictures except for the fraction of a second when a given image is registered on the retina. The moment the eyeball moves, a new image is registered, with the result that impressions recorded over a period of a few minutes become a continually changing kaleidoscope of images, colors, shapes, sizes, textures, and lines, many of which are superimposed on others or rearranged from the order in which they originally appeared. To these may be added memory, fantasy, pleasant dreams, nightmares, and personal visions. All of these make up the raw material for conceptual imagery. The individual response to them creates the unique expression that frequently results.

The fantastic creations of Hieronymus Bosch resemble nothing on this earth. His *Tree Man in a Landscape* (Fig. 25), for instance, shows a form based on a tree but with humanoid characteristics. The Tree Man is standing, for no apparent reason, in two little boats in the water, and a group of people are having dinner inside his body. On his head rests a jug, from which emerges a ladder being climbed by a tiny man. It is characteristic of Bosch's work that his inventions manage to seem at once whimsical and disquieting. All, however, are interwoven in a composition that unifies his conceptual imagery.

Now that we have explored the nature of design, we are ready to deal with the practical and specific ways of approaching the subject, both as designer and as one who uses, judges, and appreciates design. In Chapter 2 we will see how each of us is, in essence, a designer.

25

25
Hieronymus Bosch.
Tree Man in a Landscape.
c. 1500. Pen and brown ink,
10¹⁵/₁₆ × 8⅜" (27.54 × 21.59 cm).
Albertina Gallery, Vienna.

2 The Individual as Designer

Nearly everyone is a designer. We design when we plan our days with a balance of work and recreation. We design again when we organize the contents of a desk or dresser, arrange furniture or place books on a shelf in an orderly fashion. A person who hangs laundry on a line with garments grouped according to size and shape is creating a unified visual design. There is no better example of design than a workshop arranged with an assemblage of tools neatly placed for immediate accessibility (Fig. 26).

Design by Selection

We are also continual *critics* of design. Every time we make a purchase from among a selection of items we exercise judgment in matters of appearance and function.

For fifty thousand years people have used a sharp edge for cutting. Today we select our cutting edges from hundreds of varieties of scissors and knives. The knives differ in width and length of blade, in size, shape, and material of handle, and in the potential for retaining a keen cutting edge without continual sharpening. Even the choice of a knife for kitchen use presents a formidable exercise in selection (Fig. 27). The choice of a vessel for drinking means choosing from hundreds of possible designs,

26

27

26
Workshop of E. L. Walker.
Renton, Washington.

27
Selection of kitchen knives.

28

29

ranging from traditional forms seasoned by centuries of use (Fig. 28) to models that are frankly contemporary (Fig. 29). Each choice involves judgment of available models to find the one that best suits a particular need.

When we select home furnishings, clothes, or a car, we do not make a simple choice of an individual object. Consciously or not, we are choosing an element of our personal world, a symbol of who we are and how we want to live. Every selection contributes to the design of our way of life, from the style of furniture to the colors on the walls. The relative emphasis we place on appearance or practicality provides a basic clue to our personality. Even more intimately, our clothes indicate a personal style, a costume for the role we play. Here again, durability and ease of upkeep are variable considerations, depending upon our needs, our financial capabilities, and our outlook. In the selection of a car the priorities may be reversed. Most people hope first for maximum dependability and economy of operation, yet want a model and color they can enjoy. In every choice we make, we are exercising design preferences. This selective process is very much like the first step in *creating* a design.

The Design Process: Problem Solving

The most original designs are conceived intuitively, yet the complete design process is both conscious and unconscious. Intuition presents a concept that sparks the designer's interest, and then the mind enters the

28
Egyptian Lotiform Cup.
19th–20th Dynasty Faïence.
Metropolitan Museum of Art,
Carnarvon Collection
New York (gift of Edward S.
Harkness, 1926).

29
Contemporary wine goblets.

Plate 1
Georgia O'Keeffe. *White Trumpet Flower*. 1932. Oil on canvas, 30 × 40"
(76 × 102 cm). San Diego Museum of Art (gift of Mrs. Inez Grant Parker).

Plate 2
Jane Hamilton-Merritt. *Night Fighting: South
Vietnam*. 1969. Photograph.

Plate 3
Richard Anuszkiewicz.
Blue to Red Portal. 1977.
Screenprint on Masonite, 7 × 4′
(2.1 × 1.2 m). Courtesy Editions
Lassiter-Meisel, New York.
Collection of the artist.

31

30

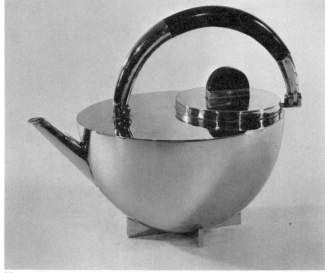

32

30
Anne Currier. *Teapot with Two Cups.* 1975.
Slip-cast earthenware with slab-built
handles and spout, luster glaze; height 9″
(22.86 cm). Courtesy the artist.

31
Wilhelm Wagenfeld. *Teapot.* 1932.
Heat-resistant glass, height 4⅜″
(11.43 cm.) Mfr.: Jensor Glaswerk
Schutt & Gen, Germany. Museum of
Modern Art, New York (gift of Philip
Johnson and Fraser's Inc., New York).

32
Marianne Brandt. *Teapot.* 1924.
Nickel silver and ebony, height 3⅝″
(8.89 cm.) Mfr.: Bauhaus Metal Workshop,
Germany. Museum of Modern Art,
New York (Phyllis B. Lambert Fund).

process by sorting out the possible approaches. Even the most seemingly
straightforward design presents a wide range of possibilities.

If the object to be designed is a teapot, for instance, one might think
there are few decisions to be made. Over the centuries, the teapot shape
has assumed a fairly standard form, determined by the requirements for
brewing and serving tea. It must be a hollow container with a lid and have
a spout for pouring, a handle, and often a strainer for the tea leaves. The
aim of a new design, however, is to create something different from what
existed before—a more beautiful or interesting appearance, a more functional shape.

One of the first decisions in designing a teapot would concern the material. Traditionally most teapots are ceramic, which holds the heat well (Fig.
30). Some, however, are glass, allowing one to watch the brewing process
(Fig. 31). A teapot can also be metal, as many fine ones have been (Fig.
32). The spout should pour without dripping or spilling: a straight or
curved spout will do this equally well. Frequently the handle reaches
across the top of the pot, but if the overall form is carefully balanced, it can
be placed on the side. Teapots generally have flat bottoms, but since they
are rarely used directly on the stove, this is a matter of tradition rather than
of function. A built-in stand to insulate the table from heat might be a
practical innovation. There remains the potential for decoration, in which
the choices are even wider. Through the creative process, the designer
seeks entirely new solutions.

We mention the possibilities above to emphasize the fact that creating a

21   *The Individual as Designer*

33

design is not a mysterious process. It is instead a series of choices similar to those we make every day. Designers approach the choices in a variety of ways. A weaver sees a skein of beautiful fiber and envisions a design to make the most of the texture and color. At another time the same weaver may want to create a runner for a table in a specific room and will set about finding appropriate fibers to complement the setting. An interesting block of wood has inspired many an artist to find a use that would exploit the grain (Fig. 33), whereas a commission for a chest or wall panel will necessitate searching for the proper wood to fulfill the purpose. Design evolves in many ways.

Scientists and engineers pursue results through orderly processes, usually based on mathematics. Art is considered to be more intuitive in nature, yet the process of design follows orderly procedures not unlike those used in the sciences. In either case, the development of a solution is fundamentally a matter of *problem solving.*

Expert problem solvers in all fields appear to work through certain mental stages. These stages, the steps in any creative work, could be identified as *definition, creativity, analysis, production,* and *clarification.* The stages do not necessarily occur in a fixed sequence but are named primarily for the purpose of identifying a mental attitude at a specific point in the development of a work.

There are many ways of approaching the *definition* of a problem. Some people use diagrams and sketches, laying out aspects of the problem in visual symbols. In designing the teapot mentioned already, for instance, one might sketch the essential elements simply as diagrams of what is involved. Next, one would visualize the working process—the finished object in use and the demands that would be made upon it. These could be set down in a few phrases beside the sketches. A methodical person might jot down the word "Given" and list the essential needs, then the word "Find" with the solutions to be worked out listed under it. As a starting point, the definition of the problem can be a reassuring step, helping the solver to be emotionally calm, confident, and creative. Two interior designers make statements that can help us to understand what is involved here. Tonny Foy says: "The kind of contemporary design I do is changing the function of space . . . rearranging rooms to suit the rhythms of a person's life."[1] Designer Jay Spectre states: "Most of my interiors seem to work best at night, because they are apartments in the city and the residents are usually out most of the day."[2] Each of these designers has arrived at a basic definition of his work in general. From this point, each commission can be approached with a specific definition of the individual problem.

Creativity describes the stage at which the imagination soars. Some designers fantasize to the extreme, pushing originality beyond the obvious solutions to discover surprising results. The construction in Figure 34 is an excellent example. What might have begun as a wall hanging evolved through imaginative use of materials and forms into a unique work, one that did not simply decorate a wall but formed a dynamic wall in itself.

Analysis is the direct opposite. It means applying preset rules of judgment and taking account of constraints of time, economy, and purpose. Analysis employs logic, integrity, and the consideration of potential problems. If some aspect of the project appears to be an insurmountable

33
Tony Howard. *Spreader.* 1983. Madrona, 11¼ × 2¼" (28.58 × 5.72 cm).

34
Patricia Campbell.
Constructed Light Wall II. 1979.
Shellacked fabric, paper, cord, fabricated; 96 × 78 × 18" (2.44 × 1.98 × .46 m).
Collection of the artist.

35
Poster for Guggenheim Museum in New York. Malcolm Grear Designers.

[1]Paige Rense, "People Are the Issue," *Architectural Digest,* May 1981, p. 24.

[2]Paige Rense, "People Are the Issue," *Architectural Digest,* September 1980, p. 24.

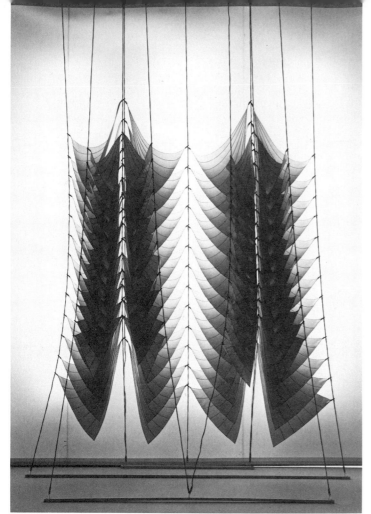

The Guggenheim Museum

34   35

problem, it helps to isolate it. When dissected and viewed from different angles, obstacles sometimes disappear; if they don't, it is at the analytical stage that the necessary adjustments can be made.

Production of a work is not simply the carrying out of decisions made through definition and analysis. Throughout the actual construction, the designer must remain flexible in order to take advantage of unexpected implications in the material or in the evolving form. It is the degree of imagination with which the necessary choices are made that determines the ultimate character of a work.

In the poster in Figure 35 the designer was working with a flat rectangle in which a circular form was to be displayed. The problem was defined as one of communication, reaching the public with a reminder that the museum was there. Basic decisions concerned scale and placement. Numerous choices were possible. A medium-size depiction of the museum would have carried the message. The type could have been superimposed upon the image or placed at the top of the rectangle. The outstanding characteristic of the building, its dramatic spiral form, was chosen as the keynote of the design. Its monumental aspect was accentuated by the use of seven simple rectangles, slightly curved, diminishing in size, and alternating in light and dark. Through them, the spiral effect directs the eye to the startlingly simple block print at the bottom. Simplicity carries a potent impact.

36

The design process is a continuous unfolding in which each step determines those that follow, culminating in *clarification.* Regardless of the designer's methods, there comes a moment when the work is done, and the effort to appraise it must be made. Occasionally, the designer is elated with the results. Sometimes, looking at one's finished work is a disappointment. This is the stage at which an artist or designer grows, becoming critic and objective appraiser of an intensely personal effort. The person who can be objective enough to analyze the strengths and weaknesses of a particular piece will strive onward in a process of continuing improvement. This is the approach of the professional designer.

Integrity of Design

The quality that makes a design a unique expression of its time and of its creator can be described as *integrity.* Stemming from the Latin *integritas,* the word *integrity* has as one of its meanings the quality or state of being whole. In design, this means a unity in the artist's conception that makes a design a personal and original statement. There are several areas in which integrity contributes to the effectiveness of a design.

Before any design can be attempted, the designer should be aware of what *materials* are available and should be familiar with their advantages and limitations. The architect must know which materials are strong in compression (when pressed under weight) and which have more strength in tension (when stretched). The sculptor should understand which materials are capable of assuming certain forms, which will endure the longest, and how they will behave when exposed to weather. Painters will be better able to achieve effects they are seeking if they are familiar with the various painting media available. They must also be aware of a medium's potential for endurance. A painting whose surface cracks or flakes after a few months of hanging on a wall does not have integrity.

36
Folding telephone by Technidyne. 1982.

37
Lynda Benglis. *Adhesive Products.* 1971.
Nine individual configurations of
black pigmented polyurethane,
13'6" × 80' × 15' (4.11 × 24.38 × 4.6 m).
Walker Art Center, Minneapolis.

Materials should be used for their own qualities and for the purposes to which they are best suited. Industrial design today relies heavily on the materials that are especially of our own age—metal, plastic, and glass. In keeping with the qualities of these smooth, sleek materials, design tends to be clean and hard-edged, with a minimum of superficial ornament (Fig. 36). Forms are likely to express the function of an object, with the material implying efficiency, a "no-nonsense" approach.

In the first uses of plastics, manufacturers imitated familiar surfaces with vinyl or melamine, advertising the advantages of increased durability and ease of upkeep. Americans walk on vinyl floors patterned to imitate the ceramic tile of Europe and set their hot kettles on counters topped with melamine grained to look like wood or leather. The intrinsic qualities of the original materials are totally lost in imitation—the earthy quality of tile, the warmth and aroma of wood, the pliancy and fragrance of leather. Furthermore, in such imitations, designers miss the opportunity to create new designs appropriate to plastic. The unique qualities of plastic have been exploited by Linda Benglis in her *Adhesive Products,* shown in Figure 37. With no attempt at practical application, she has simply shown polyurethane as a flexible, flowing substance quite unlike any of the materials with which artists have worked in the past. Her nine imaginative configurations, with their fantastic organic quality, are an eloquent expression of integrity in the use of material.

During much of the twentieth century, the idea of *integrity in form* has been summed up in the phrase "form follows function." Emerging from the writings of the nineteenth-century American sculptor Horatio Greenough, this phrase is generally attributed, however, to the American architect Louis Sullivan. The concept has long been associated with the Bauhaus, a school of design founded in Weimar, Germany, in 1919. Among the major aims of the Bauhaus program was the development of designs suitable for machine production. Its faculty and staff concentrated on architecture, textiles, furniture, and household items, paring them down to essential form so they would become a direct indication of the function

37

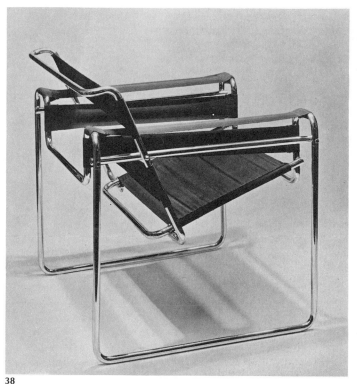

38

39

they were intended to fill (Fig. 38). Each design was to be expressive of its
material and of the machine process that made it. A chair such as the one
in Figure 38 must have seemed remarkable to the 1920s consumer accustomed to heavily carved oak and mahogany furnishings. The fact that it still
looks "modern" today testifies to its purity of design.

Design in nature adheres rigidly to the principle of form following function in the nests of birds made from materials that blend with their surroundings, thus offering protection against predators. Beavers build their
lodges from sticks and small logs under water, making it possible for them
to swim in and out and still be protected. Examples are limitless.

Along the same line, but much more elaborate, are the tree houses in
the Philippines (Fig. 39), which have been designed to cope with a hostile
climate. Deep in the jungle, in an area plagued by high humidity, floods,
insects, and dangerous animals, the tree house avoids all by its position 40
feet above the ground. This elevation also permits cooling breezes to flow
under the house. A steeply pitched roof shuns the torrential rains that are
common to this area, while minimum walls give the greatest possible ven-
tilation. Truly, function is satisfied in the form of this ingenious design.

Although form for function is most obvious in such elemental designs as
shelters, it can be equally important in more complicated ones, involving
the performance of an active task. The spinning wheel is designed for the
purpose of twisting animal, vegetable, or synthetic fibers to form threads
that can be used for weaving, knitting, or sewing. For centuries, the only
method of doing this was by twisting the fibers to be spun in one hand
while spinning with the other. The spinning wheel emerged in the eighteenth century, using the foot pedal and spindles that transformed spinning
into a smooth operation that could be accomplished by sitting at a bulky

40

41

three-legged piece of equipment. Stephen Foley has designed a contemporary version (Fig. 40) in which a delicately balanced form conserves space, and flowing lines seem a part of the act of spinning. The wheel and spindles, both circular, are the focal point, as always, but the form of the structure holding them is also curved, even where supports meet at right angles. The design and function become one.

A charming example of integrity of form can be seen in the Japanese salt basket in Figure 41. Basket weaving is an ancient craft that is still used by the Japanese for packaging. Few consumers would deny that such a package has considerably more appeal than the plastic bubble wrap so common in Western countries. The concept of a cone shape for a salt basket has a special integrity. Although it is easy to carry, this basket would not hold many apples or potatoes, for instance, and the bottom of the basket at the point of the cone would be wasted space with such cargo. Salt, however, can seep into every part of the cone, settling so the burden of weight is at the bottom; this allows for stability and total use of space. Such designs have no problems with integrity. Unhampered by distracting considerations, they provide for a need in the most direct and honest terms.

It is obvious from this discussion that, in general, integrity of form leads to integrity of *function*. The two are so interdependent that it is impossible to make a clear-cut separation between them even for purposes of discussion. Many of the irritations of modern life stem from objects lacking integrity of function. Furniture with drawers that do not run smoothly, automobiles that require a contortionist's skill to manipulate the seat belts, umbrellas that reverse under the slightest breeze—all of these are commonplace nuisances. We cannot help noting, however, that a problem with function usually stems from some fault in the form.

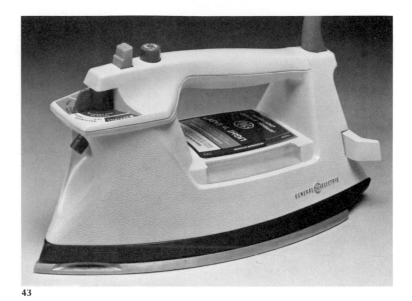

42

43

Integrity of design plays a special role when the function of an object evolves from a prototype. When electric irons were first introduced, their design remained close to the heavy flatirons that had to be heated on top of a cast iron stove (Fig. 42). It was many years before manufacturers realized that weight was no longer a factor in the effectiveness of an iron. The iron in Figure 43 is lightweight and streamlined, yet it performs its function with far less effort than its predecessor. Similar comparisons can be made with vacuum cleaners and washing machines. No longer is it necessary to bear down on a heavy machine in order to suck soil from a carpet, or to scrub violently on a corrugated metal board to keep a family in clean clothing.

The Bauhaus concept of form following function was a reaction to many centuries of ornate decoration in architecture. The name comes from the German words for *construction* and *house* and originated when Walter Gropius constructed school classrooms and dormitories in a revolutionary style of unadorned steel, concrete, and glass. More than half a century later, we are swinging back to a less austere concept of design. The movement known as Post-Modernism is bringing a return to decorative, imaginative, and emotional elements in architecture, as well as in painting, realizing that sometimes there is legitimate function in simply pleasing the eye.

Some of the best designs we see today are found in products that are uniquely of our own time, especially in the fields of communication, transportation, and sports. When a designer undertakes to create something that has never existed before, the principal concern must be with integrity of function, since there are no preconceived ideas of how such an object should look. With widespread usage the function remains important, but adjustments to weight, speed, and appearance follow quickly. We see this in radios, stereo components, television sets, and motorbikes (Fig. 44), to cite only a few examples.

No discussion of integrity in design could be complete without mention of the integrity of the designer as a person concerned with the earth and the well-being of the people who live upon it, both now and in the future. In recent years we have become aware of countless designed objects that are

42
Flatiron. 19th century.
43
Modern electric iron.
General Electric Company.
44
Suzuki GS1100ESD. 1983.

dangerous, even life-threatening. Some are the result of using dangerous materials, such as the spray cans that endanger the quality of the air we breathe, buildings containing asbestos that can cause a form of cancer, synthetic materials used in home furnishings that can bring illness to those living with them. Others are faulty in form, such as buildings that collapse, bridges that go down in storms, airplanes that crash from a malfunction, and automobiles that cause fatal accidents because of errors in construction. Thus designers have a strong responsibility for knowledge of materials and of construction principles and for a sincere concern for all people who might in any way be affected by their design. For those who are not professional designers, it is vital to be aware of materials and forms, and particularly to document unsatisfactory experiences as guidance for those responsible for designing the world in which we live.

Design is a fundamental part of environment and of living. Now that we understand its relationship to each of us as designers through selection and as consumers of designed products, it will be well to approach the methods by which designs are created.

As mentioned earlier (p. 7), design is accomplished by the use of certain *elements,* which comprise the materials with which a designer or an artist works. These elements are combined according to certain *principles.* Together the elements and principles form an aesthetic framework that is essential to any design and to any work of art, be it visual, literary, or musical. We will explore these elements and principles as they apply to visual works of art and design; first the elements—line, space, shape and mass, texture and pattern, and color. Then we will consider the ways in which these elements are combined into a design through the use of the principles of unity, variety, balance, emphasis, rhythm, proportion, and scale. All of the elements and principles interact and many are interdependent, according to their function in an individual work. This interaction forms a fascinating study, which will occupy us for the next eight chapters.

44

3 Line

The beginning of any drawing is a *point*. This is true whether it is a student's drawing, the working drawing of a professional designer, or a drawing that will ultimately become a work of art. A point is placed upon a piece of paper by a drawing tool, and the paper is no longer the same. Where that point goes can be one of the most important decisions involved in the entire work, for it is in the extension of the point, and in the determination of the direction of that extension, that *line* develops, and line is the most fundamental element of design.

Since civilization began, people have been fascinated by lines, using them to decorate primitive tools or the walls of caves. Few people can resist the urge to draw with a stick in wet sand, to doodle with a pen on paper, or to scratch with a piece of charcoal. Children draw lines on the sidewalk and invent games around them. It is almost as though it were a basic human need to draw a line, to leave one's mark.

We have mentioned lines drawn on a sheet of paper or on a canvas, but there are many kinds of lines, some created by human hands, some occurring naturally, even some that actually do not exist at all except as a consequence of human perception—a horizon line, for instance.

As an element of design, line cannot be discussed without reference to shape and space. The presence of one of these elements nearly always implies that the other two are involved. For example, a line necessarily carves out areas of space on either side of it (Fig. 45). At the same time, it is the *closure* of line that creates a shape. We cannot have shape without *edges* created by line, or without the space from which the line carves the shape. Because we recognize most things by their shapes, the lines that function as edges become particularly important. We are aware of the space within a building only because it has been demarcated by the presence of walls and a roof, in other words by the structural edges where two planes meet.

Each of these elements—line, shape, and space—is an important part of any design. Each will be discussed in a separate chapter. In this chapter we will look at the many roles line has in the visual world and at the different kinds of lines, to understand fully the possibilities of their use in the creation of designs.

Line in Nature

Lines fill every part of our world, from the dramatic line of lightning flashing across the sky to the filaments of an airborne seed (Fig. 46), from the soaring vertical lines of skyscrapers to the lines in a drawing or a painting. The natural world abounds in lines of every description.

One of the most basic natural lines is that of the human body. In a stark photograph of the Alwin Nikolais dance company (Fig. 47) our attention is directed to the line of the body in motion, extended and dramatized by lines surrounding it to create new shapes contingent upon the position of the body at any given moment. As each body moves, its surrounding lines and shapes change constantly. This use of lines to create a special choreographic effect emphasizes what every stage director or drill master knows—that the interplay of bodily lines in groups or masses can be of striking impact.

The word *line* can apply to an overall feeling or essential quality. The lines of a figure depend not only on its proportions but on the personality of

45
Aiko Miyawaki. *A Moment of Movement.*
(Utsurohi) Stainless steel wire; 1980.
12'10" × 9'6" × 13⅔" (3.9 × 3 × 4.2 m).
Collection Ichinomiya City,
Aichi Prefecture, Japan.

46
David Cavagnaro.
Thistle Seed against the Sun.
San Geronimo Valley, California.
Photograph.

47
The Nikolais Dance Theatre performing
Sanctum, with Amy Broussard, Phyllis Lamhut,
and Murray Louis.

the individual within. For instance, we have a graceful figure, a pompous figure, an athletic figure, and so on. Similarly, we speak of the majestic lines of a ship, the flowing lines of a gown, the undulating line of hills. The unique quality of an entity is expressed by the kind of *line* it presents to the human eye.

Frequently this use of line extends into symbolism. As we associate the lines of the body with different types of personality, so we may see the "sleek" lines of an aircraft not only as describing its basic form but also as hinting at its potential speed, its power, and its reflection of space-age technology.

45

46

47

48

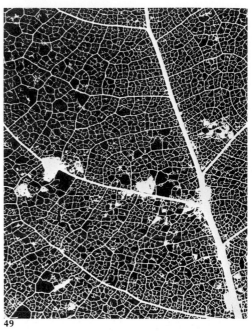

49

Nature presents an infinite variety of lines. Ripples on a pond create lines, as do grasses in a field, a pattern of pebbles on a beach, or a column of ants marching to their nest. The branches of bare trees trace magnificent patterns against a winter sky (Fig. 48), and the fallen leaf attacked by parasites exposes its own pattern of linear beauty (Fig. 49). The lines in Figure 50 change with the winds, varying from knife-edged outlines to smooth ripples extending in both directions. The curving lines of dunes terminate the long vertical line, and the strong horizontal background line is formed by mountains in the distance. If we study the world around us, we will find a wealth of natural lineal configurations.

Abstract Lines

48
David Cavagnaro. *Valley Oak, Quercus lobata, in a Winter Morning Ground Fog, near El Verano, California.* Photograph.

49
Wolf Strache. *Leaf Skeleton of Black Poplar.* 1956. Photograph.

50
Charles Moore. *Death Valley.* 1970. Photograph.

51
Facsimile of autograph manuscript of Ludwig van Beethoven's *Missa Solemnis,* page 25. Published by Hans Schneider (Tutzing).

No line of itself is abstract. A drawn line is essentially a symbol, as lines in nature are formed by human perception. In the third century B.C. Euclid used lines to develop the science of geometry, connecting points to develop theorems. Such lines are still used in engineering to calculate distances and elevations. We also use lines to plot the projected course of a spaceship. We use the term *abstract* for such lines because they are not actually visible until they are projected as symbols of knowledge we are attempting to determine or explain.

The term *abstract* may also be applied to lines that are visible only momentarily, such as those created in the water by the wake of a ship or in the sky as the jet trail that streaks behind a plane and then vanishes. The modern camera has provided us with the means of giving lasting form to abstract lines created by motion and energy. The striking linear design in Plate 2 (p. 19) was created by fighter planes in night combat over Vietnam, which the photographer caught in a long exposure.

Line as Symbol

A line becomes a *symbol* when a specific meaning is attached to it. As a symbol, it may delineate a shape that has meaning to the viewer, or it may express the reaction of the artist to the shapes, forms, and rhythms that he or she sees. Many lines do both. When two or more people agree about the meaning, the symbol can serve as a method of communication.

Sometimes the shortest lines have the most comprehensive symbolism. The lines that form letters and numbers can, in combination, represent all the knowledge that humanity has ever recorded. The symbolism of line encompasses not only all the alphabets of the world but mathematical formulas and musical scores as well (Fig. 51). Without such symbols we could not efficiently store or transmit knowledge.

50

51

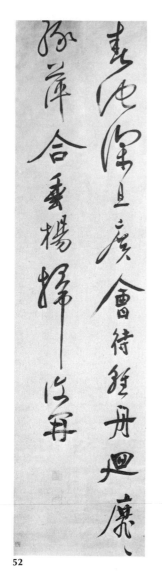

With its branches,

trunk,

and roots,

here is—

A TREE;
WOOD

"One tree does not make a
forest."

A FOREST;
A GROVE

DENSE;
THICK WITH TREES

Man plucked with his hand

two leafy branches.

52   **53**

52
Hai Jui (Chinese, 1514–87).
Hanging scroll, India ink on paper;
6'10⅞" × 1'8" (2.11 × .5 m).
Collection John M. Crawford, Jr., New York.

53
Evolution of Chinese written characters from
symbolic representations of actual objects.

54
Colin Cole, age 5.
Amy by the Gumball Machine at King Soopers.
Felt-tip pen drawing.

55
Lewis Knauss. *Rain on the Mediterranean.*
1981. Woven pile, knotted and tied;
hemp twine, linen, paint; 36 × 46"
(.92 × 1.17 m). Collection of the artist.

Nearly all civilizations have practiced a form of *calligraphy* (from the Greek for "beautiful writing"). Some of the most decorative calligraphy exists in the highly stylized brushstrokes of Oriental characters (Fig. 52). The Chinese or Japanese calligrapher is considered a master artist, who may spend years—even decades—perfecting the technique. Each element of the craft is ritualized, including the way the brush is held, the relationship of the hand to the paper, the preparation of the ink, and especially the movement of the brush's tip onto the paper and away from it.

The letters in the Roman alphabet that we use can be considered arbitrary symbols, for they are assigned to particular sounds in spoken language but have no visual meaning of their own. This is not true, however, of many forms of Oriental writing, which are *ideographic*. This means that the characters are abstracted images of what they represent; for example, the character that stands for "tree" is based on the form of a tree (Fig. 53).

Children are natural users of symbols. They will cover a sheet of paper with lines undecipherable to the adult eye and be able to explain each one. An entire experience can be translated into line (Fig. 54).

Line used as symbol becomes a powerful tool for the designer, for it permits the communication of abstract ideas or of immensely complicated associations with just a few lines or shapes. The fiberwork in Figure 55 depends on its linear quality for both symbolism and visual impact. A linear design without symbolism can be visually pleasing, but a design that makes use of symbols, whether they are personal, general, or universal, makes a much stronger impression on the viewer.

54

55

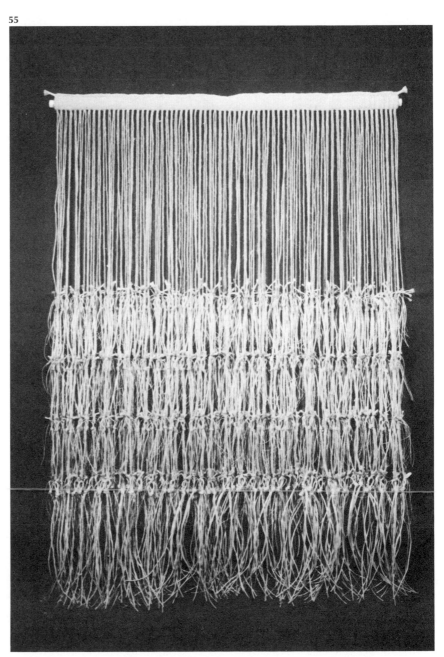

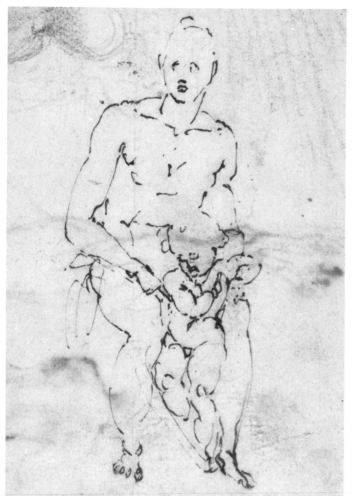

57

56

Line as Contour and Modeling

A contour line is a line that traces outline or overall shape. Existing on a two-dimensional surface, it does no more than carve that surface into two-dimensional shapes. In the hands of a skilled artist, however, a contour line can give a distinct sense of three-dimensional volume. The sketch in Figure 56 is a sketch that Michelangelo did while planning a sculpture to be executed in stone. It is interesting to note that the broken line is just as effective as a continuous one would be in delineating the forms of the figures, and at the same time, it seems to convey by its staccato character the action of the chisel as it will gouge into the stone.

The artist who wishes to convey more specifically the details of surface, feature, or different planes may use a *modeled line*. Such a line can be shaded, perhaps with the side of a pencil or a smudge of charcoal, or there may be closely spaced parallel lines (hatchings) or intersecting parallel hatchings (cross-hatchings) to mold the two-dimensional surface into a variety of planes and hollows (Fig. 57).

Line as Form

Sometimes line does not merely convey form but actually *is* form. We see this most readily in three-dimensional works such as sculpture or constructions, where wires and fibers are the means of building form. Alberto Giacometti's *Chariot* (Fig. 58) is really nothing more than an assembly of lines, in this case drawn in bronze. The subject matter is obvious, nevertheless, even the simplified figure of the charioteer.

58

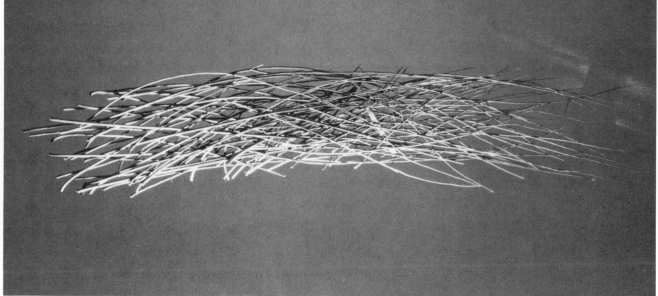

59

Concerned with the rhythms of the natural environment and the universal life force, Carol Shaw-Sutton has constructed a series of "space drawings," using the sucker shoots of willow and wild plum. These shoots build a linear construction composed of layers suggesting depths and ripples, with which she intersperses linen threads and washes of color. In *Dusk River Crossing* she seeks to express a personal experience by means of an intricate construction of lines (Fig. 59).

Light is an important tool in any area of design. Otto Piene uses it in polyethylene tubing for his *Manned Helium Sculpture* in Figure 60. The movement of the lines, with their highlights and gradations of color and shadow, becomes a kind of symbolic choreography in which the human eye continues the movement, arousing in the viewer a wealth of personal associations.

In Steven Weiss' table in Figure 61 the lines are actually the perimeters of sheets of Plexiglas cut in such a way that their edges catch the light. In a sense this work could be seen as an example of lines that do not actually exist, yet the lines are like the forms in Michelangelo's sculpture (Fig. 13) in that they are within the material, waiting for the imaginative artist to release them. Under proper lighting conditions, everything disappears except the tabletop and the compositions of lines supporting it, producing the dramatic illusion of a form that is purely linear.

59
Carol Shaw-Sutton. *Dusk River Crossing.*
1981. Fruitwood, linen, paint;
20 × 94 × 4" (50.8 × 238.76 × 10.16 cm).
Collection of Gary Austin.

60
Otto Piene. *Manned Helium Sculpture
Stage 1* from *Citything Sky Ballet.* 1970.
Helium-filled polyethylene tubing.
Courtesy the artist.

61
Steven Weiss.
"Infinity" table. Plexiglass.

62
Crystal glassware in the "twist" pattern,
designed by Michael Boehm for
Rosenthal Studio-Linie. 1973.

Line as Pattern or Texture

When lines are drawn close together or when similar lines are repeated in a composition, they may create a visual pattern or texture. We noted the use of closely placed lines to achieve modeling in the head in Figure 57.

Lines as decorative design are used in many different media. In a set of glasses designed by Michael Boehm (Fig. 62), a pattern of thin lines swirls upward in a diagonal movement from the base of each glass to the rim. The delicate linear design helps to emphasize the swell of the forms. The lines formed by a potter's fingers in throwing a clay pot provide the same kind of decorative design, as do the lines of a woodcarver's chisel.

60

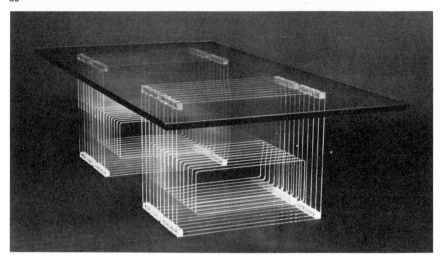

61
62

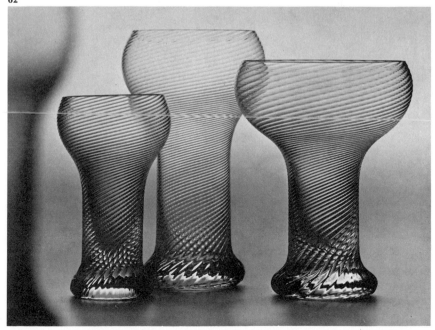

63

Line as Direction and Emphasis

In any design, line can perform the important function of leading the eye and creating emphasis. Figures 63 and 64 show opposite aspects of the way in which line can lead the eye. In the painting by Al Held (Fig. 63), lines and forms are carried to the edge of the canvas and then chopped off abruptly so that the viewer's eye is continually pulled *out* of the painting and back *in* again. The impression is of an infinitely expanding universe. By contrast, the lines in Amédée Ozenfant's *Fugue* (Fig. 64) all curve inward and are contained by a basically rectangular format. Their swelling and tapering widths encourage us to follow them around in their rhythmic paths throughout the drawing. There is nothing static about this work; the lines keep our eyes moving continually. While it is obvious that the work depicts a collection of distinctive shapes, the lines become so dominant that the rhythm created by the flowing and interaction of the shapes seems far more important than the shapes themselves.

Line plays an important part in any *composition*. We use the term to mean the total structure or organization of any work of art or design, whether it is a drawing, a pot, or a building. In the painting in Figure 65, line is used to awaken an emotional response in the viewer. The entire composition seems in repose—the horizontal lines of clouds, the slightly swelling ground, the distant horizon. Even the tiny vertical accents of trees, steeples, and human figures are located in such a way that two horizontal lines could be drawn across their tops. The strong contrast in darks and lights keeps the work from being monotonous and at the same time provides a sense of distance. It is the lines of the work that give it the predominant feeling of early evening quiet. Here the element of time enters in. We do not devote a separate chapter to *time*, but it must be understood as an important component of any composition, for it is time that makes possible our awareness of the various aspects of the work and our ultimate emotional reaction to it.

63
Al Held. *Noah's Focus I.* 1970. Acrylic on canvas, 11'6" × 2'1" (3.51 × .64 m). Courtesy André Emmerich Gallery, New York.

64
Amédée Ozenfant. *Fugue.* 1925. Pencil, 18 × 22" (45.72 × 55.88 cm). Museum of Modern Art, New York (gift of the artist).

65
Caspar David Friedrich. *The Evening Star* (Der Abendstern). c. 1825. Oil on canvas, 12½ × 17½" (31.75 × 44.45 cm). Freies Deutsches Hochstift, Frankfurter Goethe-Museum.

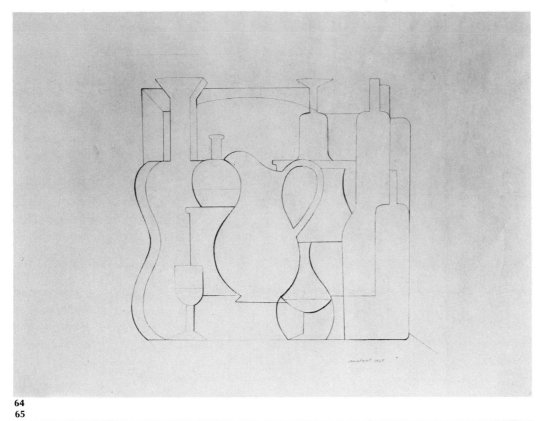

64
65

66

The Quality of Line

We have discussed a variety of lines—thin and thick, dark and light, straight and swirling. In the works by Held and Ozenfant (Figs. 63 and 64) the lines were deliberately varied to suggest contour, form, swelling, and shadow. This is what we mean by the *quality* of line.

One of the masters in the use of line was Katsushika Hokusai, a Japanese artist who lived in the late eighteenth and early nineteenth century. Known widely for his color woodcuts, Hokusai also produced an impressive group of drawings in which he used line in a dramatic manner reminiscent of the woodcut technique. In Figure 66, for example, his line, though it is always strong, varies in width from a fine line, which gives a humorous twist to a foot, to a broad, angular line, which depicts descriptively the fold of a garment. These folds and shadows delineate the figures within, transmitting, through the careless disarray of clothing, the state of utter relaxation.

Dramatic use of line is not limited to drawing. The painting by Bridget Riley in Figure 67 depends entirely upon the quality of line for its effect. The variations in width of line produce an undulating surface and a strong

66
Hokusai. *A Sake Bout.* Late 18th or early 19th century. Ink on paper, 10½ × 15" (26 × 38 cm). Freer Gallery of Art, Smithsonian Institution, Washington, D.C.

67
Bridget Riley. *Drift No. 2.* 1966. Acrylic on canvas, 7'7½" × 7'5½" (2.32 × 2.27 m). Albright-Knox Art Gallery, Buffalo (gift of Seymour H. Knox).

67

sense of form and movement. This is Op Art, relying for its effect upon optical illusions resulting from the exploitation of afterimages and retinal response. In this particular case, the illusions are created entirely by lines—light lines alternating with dark lines and with a shaded area at either edge. The quality of the lines creates a vibrant continuum, of which we seem to be seeing only a segment as it billows past us.

43   *Line*

68

Vigorous, ragged, curving lines may imply terror or turbulent emotions in general, as in a drawing by Honoré Daumier (Fig. 68). For this work the artist has used line in a compelling manner to create a tremulous form that seems to be shrinking back in fear.

Another strong effect is communicated by Ronaldo de Juan's menacing drawing entitled *Gate # 6* (Fig. 69). The heavy charcoal lines at the center of the composition seem to loom threateningly, while the curving lines at the bottom suggest whiplash strokes.

In demonstrating the powerful use of line, we have used many examples of art rather than of design specifically. This will be true in our discussion of all the elements and principles, for, as we noted earlier, all works of art have a strong basis in design, and the impact of specific elements is sometimes particularly obvious in a drawing or painting. The importance of such examples is to emphasize the special quality of an element or principle of design, a quality that can be translated into specific designs once it is fully appreciated. The importance of line lies in its ability not only to convey shape but also, by its very quality, to express or arouse a mood, a strong emotion, or an impression.

68
Honoré Daumier. *Fright (L'Épouvante).*
Charcoal over pencil on paper, 8¼ × 9⅜″
(20.96 × 24.13 cm). Art Institute of Chicago
(gift of Robert Allerton).

69
Ronaldo de Juan. *Gate #6.* 1976.
Charcoal, 6′3″ × 3′10″ (1.9 × 1.16 m).
Private Collection.

4 Shape and Mass

Shape is created by closed line. The three-dimensional extension of shape is called *mass*. The terms *volume* and *form* are synonymous with mass in common usage, but since we have already noted the meaning of form as a design term, we will use mass in our discussion of the three-dimensional aspect of shape.

We can see the difference between *shape* and *mass* by referring to geometry, which distinguishes the plane geometric figures (shapes) of square, circle, and triangle from the solid geometric figures (masses) of cube, sphere, and pyramid. Just as solid geometry is a more complicated system of mathematics than plane geometry, the designer may find greater difficulty in working with three-dimensional masses than with flat shapes. This is because the lines multiply, appearing in several planes, making more involved spaces.

Perception of Shape and Mass

In perception, shape and mass are closely related. When we look at the moon we actually *see* a flat circle against a dark sky, yet we *perceive* a round mass. The same could be said for an orange or a tennis ball. Psychologists have concluded that the brain plays a large part in shape perception, in other words, that there is a conceptual element involved. What this means is that the stimulus that acts upon the eye is broken up into discontinuous parts, which are rearranged by the brain into a pattern that can be recognized. There are various theories about how this recognition takes place. One is that the brain fits the stimulus material into templates of relatively simple shape, providing the new material with structural features that have a general kind of familiarity. It is believed that actual perception involves not unique shapes but a kind of pattern to which any given shape can be fitted.

A shape becomes a mass when the eye changes position, taking in more surfaces or aspects than were originally perceived (Fig. 70). When the image of an object changes, it is necessary to understand whether the change is in the object itself or in the context in which it is seen, or in both. In our discussion of mass we will explore the ways in which artists convey three-dimensional masses on a flat surface. First, however, we will consider the possibilities of shape as an element of design.

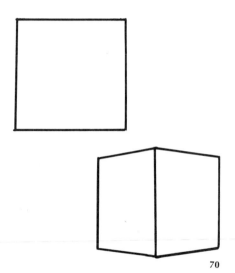

70

71

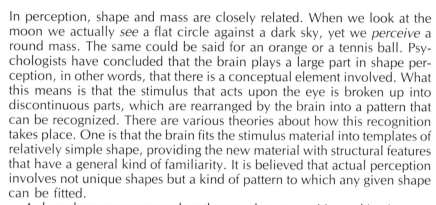

70
A square can become a cube when the viewpoint is changed.

71
Stonehenge. 1800–1400 B.C. Height of stones above ground 13′6″ (4.1 m). Salisbury Plain, Wiltshire, England.

72
Chambered nautilus (*Nautilus pompilius*) from Polynesia.

73
A microscopic view shows that cells from the cornea of an insect's eye are hexagonal.

Shape

Shapes can be divided into four broad categories: *geometric, natural, abstract,* and *nonobjective.* These are not rigid divisions but allow for some overlapping.

Geometric shapes dominate the constructed environment. They appear in buildings, bridges, furniture, and machines of all kinds. Basic *post-and-lintel construction,* which sets a horizontal crosspiece over two separated uprights to create a square shape, has been fundamental since prehistoric times. The solidity of the square has permitted the huge structures at Stonehenge to remain in position for 3500 years, despite the fact that they were erected by primitive means, with no mortar of any kind to hold them together (Fig. 71). Of course, in viewing Stonehenge in silhouette, we must realize that it is fundamentally mass, as is the case in nearly any construction. Though the stability of Stonehenge depended on the shape of the blocks of stone, its basic durability depended on their massiveness.

Industrial design depends heavily on geometric shapes, simply because they are so regular. Machines and shaping equipment can be easily adapted to these precise outlines. Besides this, many considerations of function and storage demand geometric shape. A record must be round to revolve on a turntable, but the record-album cover, being square, allows for convenient storage. Gears must be round, whether in automobiles or watches, since their function depends upon the ability to turn. We could give hundreds of such examples.

We often think of geometric shapes as having been invented by humans, but of course many geometric shapes exist in nature. We can find the square in mineral crystals, the triangle in certain leaf shapes, the circle developed to a spiral in a shell formation (Fig. 72). Microscopic views often reveal nearly perfect geometric shapes in unexpected places; Figure 73 shows row upon row of hexagons—complex geometric shapes—in an insect's eye.

72

73

74

74
Harijan patchwork quilt. Embroidered
and pieced cotton, 6'9¼" (2.06 m).
From Kutch district of India.
UCLA Museum of Cultural History.
Gift of Mr. and Mrs. Richard B. Rogers.

75
Frank Stella. *Moultonville III.* 1965–66.
Enamel on canvas, 10'4" × 7'2"
(3.15 × 2.18 m). Nelson Gallery, Atkins
Museum, Kansas City (gift of Friends of Art).

76
Japanese stencil used to decorate silk.
c. 1680–1750, Tokugawa period. Slater
Memorial Museum, Norwich Free Academy,
Norwich, Conn., Vanderpoel Collection.

Designs from early periods of civilization or from remote areas of the world frequently have a predominantly geometric theme. American Indian designs on pottery, baskets, and rugs are almost always geometric symbols of natural forces. The quilt in Figure 74, composed entirely of squares and variations on the triangle, is from the dowry of a woman in Kutch, a region on the west coast of India.

Many twentieth-century artists have felt that geometric shapes and masses are appropriate expressions of a highly mechanized and technical civilization. Richard Anuszkiewicz executed a series of prints based on designs created from the rectangle. Although the elements are simple— concentric rectangles and straight lines—the results have a dynamic quality. In Plate 3 (p. 20) there is warmth and movement, the result of careful variation in the placement of the lines and of subtle gradations of color in the rectangular bands.

Frank Stella carried geometry even further. The canvases for a series of paintings were stretched on geometric frames that are, instead of conventional rectangles, circles, tilted rectangles, pentagons, and other more intricate shapes. By emphasizing the irregular shape of the canvas, the painting in Figure 75 manages to make the flat surface look three-dimensional through a *trompe l'oeil* (fool-the-eye) effect.

As noted above (Figs. 72 and 73), many shapes found in nature are geometric. *Natural shapes* are generally understood to include human, animal, and plant shapes, and the scope of their interpretation is immense. The Japanese silk design in Figure 76 could have been derived from either flowers or snowflakes or both; its charm lies in the originality that brings both basic forms together into a new and decorative design. The design of

75

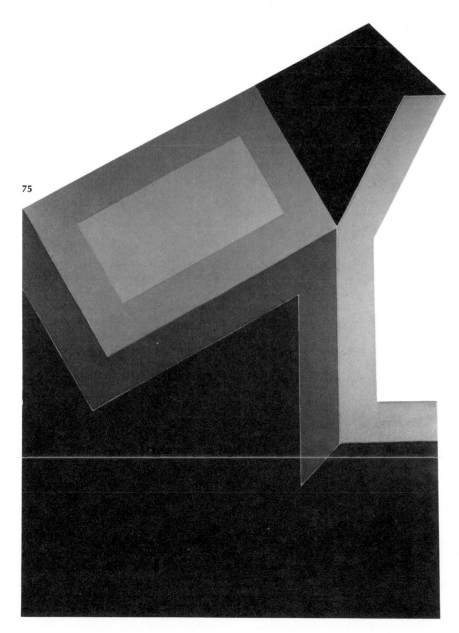

76

77

the cotton print from Finland (Fig. 77) looks like a huge flower form, yet its title suggests that the artist had something else in mind. In either case, the inspiration is from nature and the interpretation original and dramatic.

The sinuous forms found in nature were one of the inspirations for an art movement that flourished around the turn of this century. Now generally known by its French name, *Art Nouveau,* it had various names in Europe and took many forms. One of the most original proponents of this movement was the Spanish architect Antoni Gaudí, who designed buildings to look like organic botanical entities that grow and proliferate before our eyes. His cathedral of the *Sagrada Familia* in Barcelona is still under construction (Pl. 4, p. 53).

77
Medusa. Screened cotton print by Maija Isola for Marimekko, Helsinki.
78
Tak Kwong Chan. *The Horse—Away He Goes.* 1980. Brush and ink, 24 × 40″ (.61 × 1.02 m). Collection of the artist.

While plant shapes lend themselves to a variety of interpretations, animal shapes are often used with a touch of whimsy. Many centuries before Christ, artists were painting or carving on walls the images of animals—bulls, cats, deer, and many varieties of birds—with almost modern stylization and often with a touch of humor. Contemporary artist Tak Kwong Chan, with a few masterful brush strokes, creates horses that are full of action and beauty. Like so many works by Chinese artists, his paintings are striking designs as well as forceful paintings (Fig. 78).

When a natural shape is distorted in such a way as to reduce it to its essence, we say that it has been *abstracted*. This means that, though the source of the shape is recognizable, the shape has been transformed into something different. Usually, this is done by simplification, by omitting all nonessential elements. A series of lithographs by Picasso, taken from an edition of eighteen, will illustrate the principle of abstract shapes.

78

The fifth print (Fig. 79) shows a fairly "natural" representation of two female nudes. Except for some distortion of the eyes and nose on the figure at left, the drawing seems lifelike, with normal shapes and volumes. By the tenth state (Fig. 80) Picasso has begun to abstract many of the elements in the drawing. Both figures are flattened, particularly the one at left, and the face at left has been drastically simplified into a circle with angular features. The left background form, which in the earlier print was a conventional suggestion of architectural space, has become a geometric screen.

By the seventeenth state (Fig. 81), the composition has been highly abstracted. Both figures are transformed into flat collections of shapes. The face at left is a primitive mask, while the one at right has all but disappeared. Breasts are circles or simple curves. Fingers and toes now resemble oversize flattened cylinders. If we had only this print to look at, we would identify it as two female nudes, but we could not see how Picasso arrived at this particular interpretation. By comparing the three states we can follow his investigation of certain shapes, planes, and outlines that fascinated him. The abstraction is not arbitrary but a systematic development from the representational drawing.

79

80

81

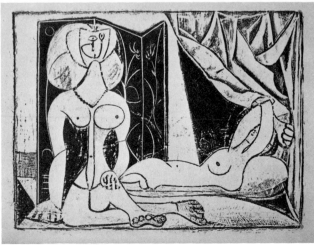

79
Pablo Picasso. *Les Deux Femmes Nues*
(Two Nude Women). 1945–46. Lithographs,
eighteen states, each c. 10⅛ × 13⁵⁄₁₆"
(25.65 × 34.04 cm). Cleveland Museum of Art
(J. H. Wade Fund). State V.

80
State X.

81
State XVII.

Plate 4
Antoni Gaudí. *La Sagrada Familia,* Barcelona. Begun 1903;
work terminated 1926 and resumed 1952; still under construction.

Plate 5
Rembrandt. *The Descent from the Cross*. 1651. Oil on canvas, 4'8½" × 3'7¾" (1.43 × 1.11 m).
National Gallery of Art. Washington, D.C. (Widener Collection).

82

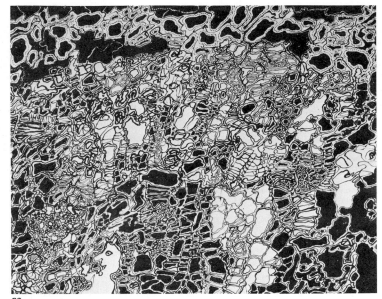

83

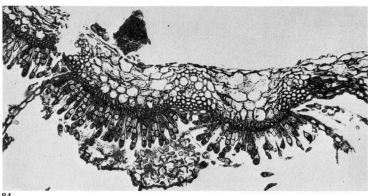

84

Abstraction has long been one of the most effective means of communication, as we mentioned in connection with the symbolism of written characters (p. 33). The United States is now adopting some of the abstract highway signs that have long provided a common language for motorists in Europe. Despite the different languages spoken in European countries, drivers are able to interpret directions and warnings with no difficulty. Although American drivers speak and read a common language, the abstract pictures are more eloquent and easier to grasp than printed words, especially when seen from a moving vehicle (Fig. 82).

Shapes that do not relate to anything in the natural world are termed *nonobjective.* This is really a comparative term, because it is virtually impossible to create shapes that no one will find familiar in some way through perceptual associations. Jean Dubuffet undoubtedly was working for fantasy in his drawing *Radieux Météore* (Fig. 83) since the title (Radiant Meteor) is of a subject unseen by the human eye. It is interesting that a similar configuration can be found in nature, not in the sky but as a parasite in a wheat field (Fig. 84). Nevertheless, Dubuffet's work would be categorized as nonobjective since that was the artist's intent.

85

A painting by Joan Miró in Figure 85 demonstrates the way in which *shape relationships* interact. Miró has combined highly abstracted shapes of human heads and features with a network of geometric and nonobjective shapes. Unity in the composition is achieved by the general similarity among the various types of shapes. The dark circle that is an eye in one place becomes elsewhere just a circle or is distorted into a blob. Pattern is created by a rhythm of outlined and filled-in shapes, of light and dark. In other words, Miró has built his composition from shape relationships.

In *The Swimming Pool,* Henri Matisse abstracts human figures to interact with the water in which they are moving (Fig. 86). The figures have become so abstract, in fact, that, in many cases, they lose their original similarity to the human body. Matisse's purpose was not so much to represent swimmers as to show the pool and the shapes within it as a single entity, moving, diving, and surfacing.

Another important relationship is that between shapes within a composition and the shape of the *field* or *ground*—that is, the canvas, page, or external outline. Many of the works of Josef Albers are a series of squares related to a square field (Fig. 87). As we will see in Chapter 7, Albers was greatly concerned with the interaction of color, and his compositions with their sensitively proportioned squares provide ideal vehicles for experiments with variations in color combinations.

85
Joan Miró. *The Beautiful Bird Revealing the Unknown to a Pair of Lovers.* 1941. Gouache and oil wash, 18 × 15″ (45.72 × 38.1 cm). Museum of Modern Art, New York (Lillie P. Bliss Bequest).

86
Henri Matisse. Three panels from *The Swimming Pool,* a nine-panel mural in two parts. 1952. Gouache on cut-and-pasted paper mounted on burlap, 7′6⅝″ × 27′9½″ (2.3 × 8.47 m) and 7′6⅝″ × 26′1½″ (2.3 × 7.96 m). Museum of Modern Art, New York (Mrs. Bernard F. Gimbel Fund).

87
Josef Albers.
Homage to the Square: Silent Hall. 1961. Oil on composition board, 40″ (1.02 m) square. Museum of Modern Art, New York (Dr. and Mrs. Frank Stanton Fund).

86
87

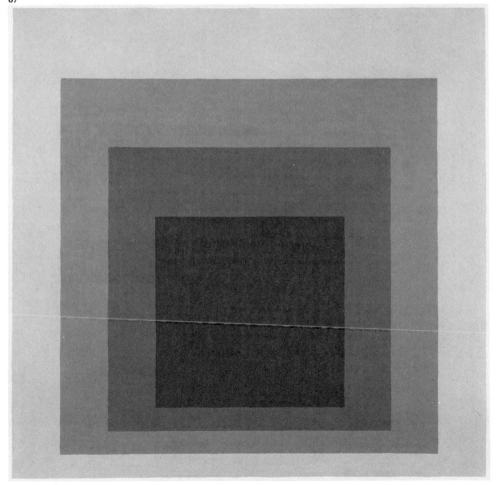

57   *Shape and Mass*

88

89

Mass

The categories that we identified in shape apply to mass as well. On a flat surface, shape becomes mass through illusion as a result of various devices of the artist, such as shading or the use of perspective. *Actual mass* is one of the most important elements of design.

Geometric masses—the cube, sphere, and pyramid—are the three-dimensional equivalents of the square, circle, and triangle. To these we must add the cone (a triangle rotated on its axis) and the cylinder (a rectangle rotated on its bisector).

A cube may be the most visually stable of all forms. However, it need not always be so. The sculptor Isamu Noguchi sets us on our ears, so to speak, by tipping his cube up on one corner (Fig. 88). The lines of this work, which would otherwise have been placid verticals and horizontals, now become energetic diagonals thrusting upward. This cube makes an effective counterpoint to the conventional cube of the skyscraper behind it.

Just as a cube is normally a restful mass, the sphere is somehow a *satisfying* mass. Globes, rubber balls, and the earth itself—all are spheres. Most people, when they pick up a lump of clay or dough, automatically form it into a sphere. The glass sculpture in Figure 89, shimmering with light, is made in the form of an "earth satellite." Even while it rests on its pedestal, we can imagine this airy form beginning to lift upward and hover in the air, gently spinning as it goes. This idea expresses one of the most intriguing characteristics of the sphere. It seems ever mobile, always turning, never static. There are no sharp edges to bring motion to a halt, as there are in a cube. A sphere nearly always implies movement and time.

88
Isamu Noguchi. *Cube.* 1969. Steel and aluminum, painted and welded, height 28′ (8.53 m). Located in front of 140 Broadway, New York.

89
Pavel Hlava (in cooperation with the workshop of Miroslav Lenc, Czechoslavakia). *Satellite.* 1972. Blown crystal hemispheres joined by welding, diameter 13¾″ (34.93 cm). Courtesy the artist.

90
Magician's Pyramid, Uxmal, Yucatán, Mexico.

91
Mount St. Helens, Washington. May 18, 1981.

With the pyramid form, we again return solidly to earth. The pharaohs of Egypt built their burial pyramids to last for all time, and indeed they have withstood more than four thousand years of climate, wars, pillage, and geological upheaval. Many early civilizations constructed pyramids, from the first known residents of the Middle East and Southeast Asia to the Indians of pre-Columbian America (Fig. 90). While the cube is the most visually solid mass, the pyramid is immensely stable from an engineering point of view. Stresses beginning at the tip spread out in all directions to the broad base. It is no accident that these structures have outlasted all the other wonders of the ancient world.

The cone appears by nature to be a *thrusting* mass, as in the nose cone of a spaceship or the cone of a volcano. While the form of a cone may be just as firmly rooted in earth, we somehow expect something to be coming *out* of it. A volcano, even a dormant one, remains mysterious. At any time it could erupt, spewing smoke and ash and lava over the countryside (Fig. 91). Similarly, the Indian tepee, one of the most portable habitations ever invented, was planned with a hole in the center to permit the escape of smoke from the cooking fire.

90

91

92

Finally, the cylinder is a generally utilitarian mass. Cans, tubes, vases, cooking pots, cups, and many machine parts take the form of cylinders (Fig. 92). In purely practical terms the cylinder functions well because it can contain a great deal yet has no corners or crevices. We can even visualize the human body as a collection of rough cylinders, one for the trunk and one each for the limbs. The painter Fernand Léger developed this idea during the early twentieth century (Fig. 93). At the beginning of the modern industrial age, many artists celebrated the coming of machine technology. Léger abstracted portions of the human anatomy—legs, arms, fingers, toes—into precision-formed cylinders, thus emphasizing the merger between human intellect and mechanical power.

Perhaps the most obvious use of natural masses in art is sculpture of the human form, an area of design that has flourished for four thousand years. Beginning with stiff symbolic representations among primitive people, the art of figurative sculpture reached a height in the hands of the Greeks of the fourth century B.C. and their works have inspired sculptors ever since (Fig. 94). Throughout the ages, sculptures of animals have also played an important part in human expression.

93

94

PROGRESSIVE ABSTRACTION.

95

95
Henri Matisse. *Heads of Jeannette.*
1910–13. Bronze, heights 10⅜ to 24⅛″
(26.42 to 61.2 cm). Los Angeles County
Museum of Art (gift of the Art Museum
Council in memory of Penelope Rigby, 1968).

96
Marvin Lipofsky. *California Storm Series.*
1942. Blown glass, 11½ × 13″
(27 × 33.02 cm).
Collection of Samuel Budwig, Jr., Chicago.

The abstract masses in the series of heads by Matisse shown in Figure 95 recall the progressive abstraction in the Picasso prints. Here we can see that the *actual,* rather than the pictorial, planes of the face and head have been abstracted increasingly as the artist's insight progressed. The first bust, at far left, probably shows most precisely the "real" appearance of the subject. But the last interpretation, at right, may in fact express the *character* of the sitter more accurately. The last bust is not pretty but in many ways is the most interesting view. As the states progress, Matisse gradually selects particular features for intensification, while others diminish in importance. By the third state the hair has collected into three lumps, and by the fifth it has receded to the back of the head. The nose gradually becomes bigger, stronger, and more prominent, while the eyes deepen and take on a hooded quality. Perhaps Matisse sought to capture the essence of this woman, or of Woman personified. Perhaps he was fascinated by the new relationships of mass (features) on the mass of the head. At its best, abstraction evokes the basic quality of a form, while distorting its contours. By definition the *abstract* concerns the *essence* of something.

Nonobjective masses do not refer to any specific recognizable form. When they *seem* organic, as though they might be part of some living thing, they are termed *biomorphic.* The glass form in Figure 96 could be some prehistoric sea creature or a resident of an undiscovered planet. It does not resemble anything known, and yet it seems alive. The power of nonobjective masses lies in their ability to evoke response in the viewer, perhaps a hundred different responses in a hundred viewers. Each person who looks at such a form brings to it special associations and experiences, which will help to give the form a personal interpretation. The artist who works in nonobjective mass invites the participation of the spectator.

96

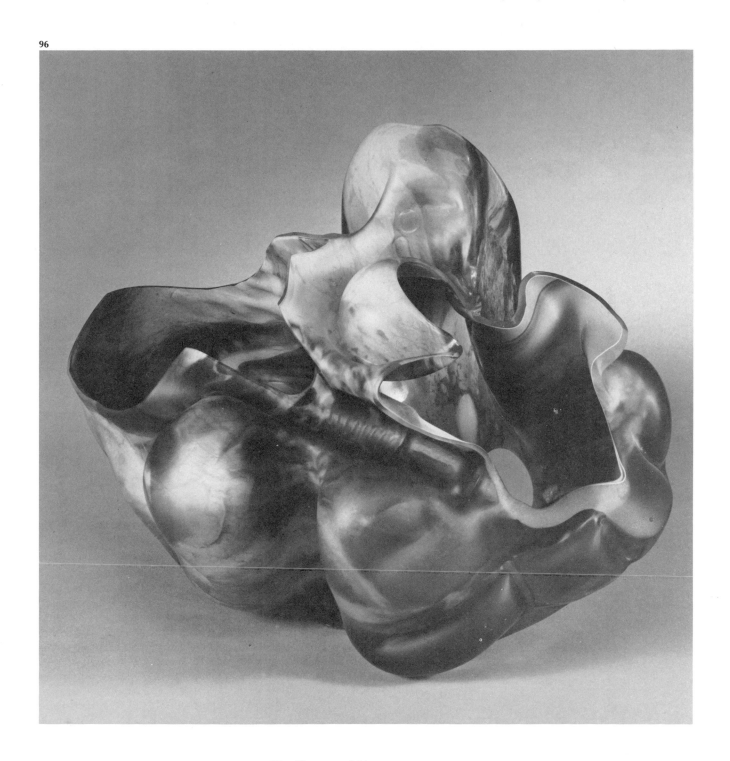

97

98

97
Russell Dixon Lamb.
Rising Wave. Photograph.

98
Pilobolus Dancers in *Monkshood Farewell.*

99
A simple line drawing of a circle when shaded can become a solid sphere.

100
A simple line drawing when shaded can become a solid geometric form.

leaves

The picture in Figure 97 shows a *moving* mass—a wave. The wave is a definite mass, yet a second after this image was captured, no single molecule of water in the wave would still have been in place, and the wave would have changed its outlines. We could point to numerous examples of this phenomenon—waterfalls, avalanches, clouds, tornadoes.

The performing arts are also concerned with mass and movement. In the dance, for instance, each dancer's body can be considered a mass—one that changes its outlines with each movement. As two or more dancers come together, they form another mass capable of transforming itself or breaking apart (Fig. 98). Each movement creates new mass and space relationships. These factors are present in a drama or a rock concert as well.

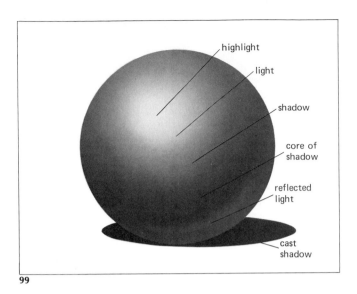

highlight

light

shadow

core of shadow

reflected light

cast shadow

99

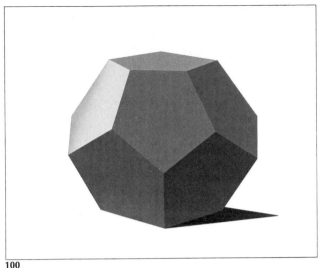

100

Converting Shape to Mass

We have implied that, generally speaking, shape is two-dimensional and mass exists in space in three dimensions. The artist also depicts three-dimensional masses on flat canvas or paper.

There are several means of achieving this phenomenon. The principal method is by shading or tonality. A circle becomes a sphere when it is shaded in a certain way (Fig. 99). A rectangle becomes a cylinder when it is shaded along the edges. A square cannot become a cube through shading alone but must be extended by means of perspective, in the same way that one's vision is extended by moving position. When a side is added to a square and shaded, a solid cube emerges. This principle can be used on any geometric mass with facets, or angular sides (Fig. 100).

Shading and tonality are basic drawing techniques. Painters use variations of these techniques by employing color and light. Grayed colors recede, so the nearest portion of a mass is made lighter. A surface catching the light emphasizes solidity and form. Darkened surfaces not only recede but turn away or under, telling the viewer the exact extent of a depicted mass. We will see examples of these devices for converting shape into mass as we study the media in which artists work. Next, however, we will explore another element that is closely associated with both shape and mass, the element of space.

5 Space

We think of space as a vast expanse in which spaceships travel millions of miles past stars and whirling planets, yet space is a vital part of even the smallest design or work of art. In creating form of any kind, one must manipulate space. The cut-paper design in Figure 101 illustrates this idea, since it can readily be seen that the design depends as much on the spaces left as on the shapes cut from the paper. In fact, if we stare at the spaces steadily, they assume a pattern of their own. In this situation, the paper pattern is known as *positive space* or pattern; the pattern left by its creation is *negative*. Continued staring may make it difficult to distinguish between the two. This phenomenon is known as *figure-ground ambiguity:* the cut paper is referred to as the *figure* and the space behind it as the *ground*. Twentieth-century painters have found this relationship especially intriguing and have made use of it in many of their works. In Figure 102, for instance, we see with one glance a classically proportioned vase. We blink our eyes and now we are looking at two profiles of Pablo Picasso, facing each other nose to nose. If we look at this work long enough, the two images (or perceptions of the image) will keep reversing, so that we alternately see one and then the other.

Psychology of Space Perception

Only a narrow range of what we see is in focus at any particular moment. When we look out over a city we feel we are seeing a panoramic view, but really our eye is capable of seeing one building at a time; the rest of the landscape is only a blur. We know the rest is there but we cannot see the details until we move our eyes. The same is true of closer range, within a room, for instance. The crystalline lens of the eye makes it necessary to select a target, a piece of furniture, a book, or a person's face, on which to concentrate our attention. This limitation is a protection rather than a handicap. The brain reacts immediately to sensory response, and if we were to be assaulted simultaneously by the details of everything around us, our intelligence would be incapable of handling all the information bombarding it. It would be like being surrounded by a crowd of people all

101

101
Christian Schwizgebel. Cut-paper silhouette from Gstaad, Switzerland. c. 1950. 11½ × 7⅔" (29 × 19.5 cm). Schweizerisches Museum für Volkskunde, Basel.

102
Jasper Johns. *Cups 4 Picasso*. 1972. Lithograph, 22 × 32" (56 × 81 cm). Universal Limited Art Editions. Courtesy Castelli Graphics, New York.

103–104
The same subject photographed with different lens settings becomes entirely different in character.

shouting at once. To bring any order out of such clamor, it is necessary to listen to one voice at a time. The need for the intelligence to sort out a point of interest is evident in our tendency to see familiar shapes in large areas over which the eye roams aimlessly. We see dragons in a bank of clouds or imagine a face in a pattern.

This principle of selective vision can be demonstrated by the camera. Standing in the same position, we have only to change the distance setting on the lens, in other words to change *focus,* to receive two entirely different images (Figs. 103—104).

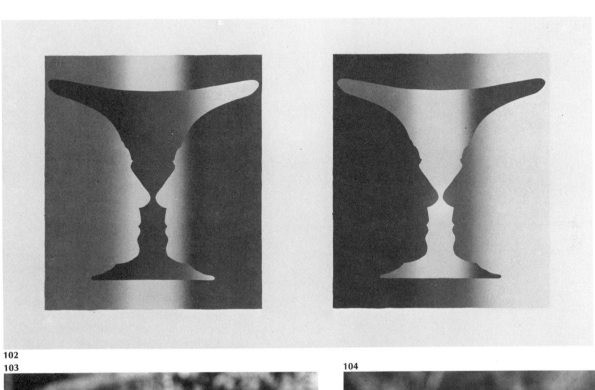

102

103

104

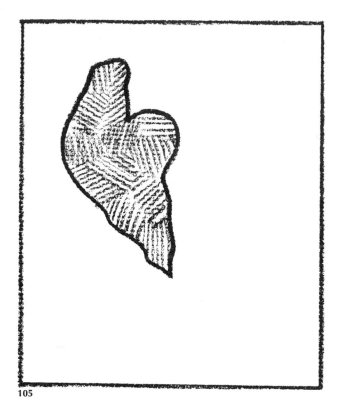

105

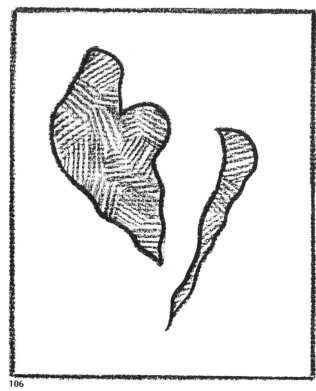

106

105
One nonobjective shape positioned in a space.

106
Two nonobjective shapes positioned in relation to one another in a space.

107
In graphic design, blocks of type become shapes to be arranged within the space of a page.

Early thinkers assumed that the object perceived actually entered the eye bodily, and they wondered how a large object could shrink to a size that could be accommodated by the small hole in the pupil of the eye. We know now that the eye receives not a part of the object itself but only an equivalent of it and the size of the image received depends upon the distance of the object from the eye. By choosing the proper distance, the viewer can make objects as big or as small as is necessary to comprehend them. A mountain does not become a mere bump because it is seen from a distance. The long range of vision reduces it to a form that can be comprehended in relationship to the vaster landscape in which it is perceived. The larger the object seen, the less of its environment will be visible. This principle is frequently used in cinematic photography. On a television or movie screen, a long-range shot is used to give the flavor of a setting or to portray people traveling over long distances. When the emphasis is on a personal reaction, however, the camera moves in to show only the person's face, excluding the setting entirely. In this way the mind of the viewer focuses on the emotional response of the actor. The attention of the audience is controlled by the photographer's manipulation of space. Each scene becomes a composition by which the photographer and director elicit a response.

The importance of space in design can be more clearly understood if we distinguish two kinds. *Actual space* is that in which a work exists. It may be the space on the two-dimensional surface of a canvas, the space occupied by a stereo component, or the three-dimensional spaces inside and around a sculpture or a building. *Pictorial space* is the illusionary space that the artist creates in a two-dimensional work, such as a drawing or a painting. This can range from a perfectly flat, patterned surface to the illusion of

deep space, as in a landscape that seems to recede into infinity. In depicting pictorial space, the artist is influenced by the psychology of space perception.

Actual Space

Anyone who works on a *two-dimensional* surface is creating an illusion. A circle becomes a ball or an apple, but it remains in reality a drawn circle. An artist or designer who is about to make the first mark on a blank canvas or piece of paper has several important decisions to make. These include not only the shape of the mark, its size, perhaps its color, but also *where the mark will be* on the canvas or paper. It may be centered, off to one side, or set high or low in the white field. Assuming for the moment a rectangular piece of paper with a *nonobjective* shape on it—a shape that does not resemble any natural form—we can see that the artist has established a *spatial relationship* between the shape and the page (Fig. 105). The shape relates to the space on all sides of it and to the rectangular field itself. This idea may seem very basic, but anyone who has ever tried to locate a shape on a blank piece of paper knows that it is not easy to find the ''best'' solution.

If the artist then introduces another nonobjective shape into the composition, the spatial relationships become more complicated (Fig. 106). Not only does each shape relate to the space of the paper, but the two shapes are related to each other in space as well. An example from graphic design may help to clarify this concept.

Let us suppose that the designer of this book, faced with a page 8¼ by 11 inches, wants to position the title of the book on that page. The words *Design Through Discovery,* set into type, constitute a black shape. The designer has almost endless choices in placing that shape, some of which are shown in Figure 107. In the end, the placement that seems most satisfying, most effective, will be the one that creates the best spatial rela-

107

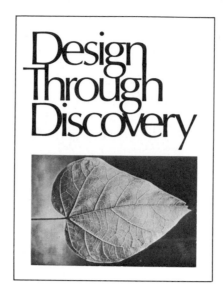

108

108
Type and illustrations combine to form
the composition of a page.
Their placement in space can affect the
sense of horizontality or verticality.

109
Henri Matisse.
The Parakeet and the Mermaid. 1952–53.
Paper cutout with gouache, 11¾″ × 25′4¼″
(3.37 × 7.73 m). Six parts.
Stedelijk Museum, Amsterdam.

110
David Smith. *Voltri Bolton VII.* 1962.
Steel, height 7′2″ (2.18 m).
Private collection.

111
Diagram of the negative spaces in
David Smith's *Voltri Bolton VII.*

tionship between the shape of the words and the space of the page. When
another shape, perhaps a photograph, must be included (Fig. 108), the
relationships multiply. The page can be made to seem more vertical or
more horizontal according to the placement of the elements, even though
all four elements are the same size.

Spatial relationships provide never-ending fascination. When, at the
end of a long and successful career as a painter, Henri Matisse became too
ill to stand before an easel, he devoted himself to cutting out abstract
shapes and experimenting with their possibilities. After having sheets of
paper painted in the colors he wanted to use, he cut, arranged, and finally
pasted the varied shapes on colored backgrounds, rearranging them endlessly until the spatial relationships were exactly as he wanted them. The
result was a series of striking designs (Fig. 109). Matisse referred to this
method of experimenting with shape and color and learning about them as

109

110

"sculpting with color." He cut away the paper in the way a sculptor chisels away stone, studying the possibilities of space and form and disposing positive and negative shapes to produce a unified result.

Sculpture and other *three-dimensional* works have always had as much to do with space as with material substance. When we look at the work in Figure 110, we see not only an assembly of forms but also a complex of spaces of different shapes. Of course, we are more aware of the positive forms than of the negative ones (or spaces), but we also cannot help taking note, perhaps unconsciously, of the latter. If we were to put a sheet of tracing paper over this photograph and fill in the spaces only, the result would look something like Figure 111—another interesting composition.

111

112

Moreover, because we are looking at a photograph, our position is fixed. If we were actually standing next to this sculpture, we would be free to move around it, and every time our viewpoint changed even slightly, the forms—*and the spaces*—would alter in shape. Clearly the sculptor must keep in mind not only the forms being created but the spaces as well, designing them from every potential vantage point.

We can experience such sculptural spaces in our parks and plazas. As spectators we can walk around such works and also under and through them, perhaps even climb upon them. This idea brings us again to the concept of *time.* It takes time to walk around and through a monumental sculpture. It also takes time to pass through a building and gradually experience its spaces. Public buildings illustrate this most clearly.

Anyone who has visited a European cathedral must recognize that a full realization of its many facets takes a great deal of time, but even the most businesslike buildings require time, to walk through halls and to find the appointed shop or office. Perhaps the most exciting experience in a public building occurs when one attends a concert or dramatic performance. The Metropolitan Opera House at Lincoln Center, like major opera houses all

112
Staircase and foyer of Metropolitan Opera House, Lincoln Center, New York.

113
Augustin Hernandez. Hernandez House, Mexico City.

114
Trumpet shell from the Philippine Islands.

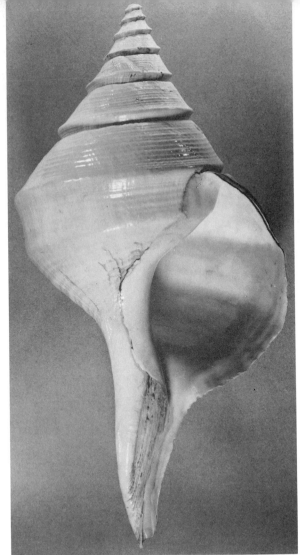

113   114

over the world, was designed to heighten the sense of anticipation by providing glamor and a sense of luxury from the moment one enters (Fig. 112). Especially at night, with the crystal chandeliers sparkling on the rich carpet and the lighted fountains shimmering outside the high windows, one lingers, climbing the staircase slowly, looking around to absorb this eloquent stage setting for the performance yet to come.

Smaller-scale architecture can also stimulate anticipation. The house in Figure 113 seems to have been sculpted rather than built, and there is a feeling of curiosity as to what the inside shapes will reveal. Its complex of shapes, curves, spaces, hollows, and projections would offer a fascinating adventure to anyone walking through. Looking at this photograph, we can see that if the photographer had stood just a few feet to either side of the present vantage point, the spaces would have changed. This house was designed for a woman who collects shells as a hobby, and its swooping curves and intersecting arcs seem to echo the configuration of a shell (Fig. 114). The element of time is essential in appreciating such a house. The viewer must linger and *experience* the spaces, feeling their flow and rhythm rather than merely viewing them.

115

Pictorial or Illusionistic Space

Pictorial space begins, and sometimes ends, with the *picture plane*—a flat surface that is synonymous with the surface of the canvas or paper being drawn upon. Artists throughout history have tried to create the illusion of "real" or three-dimensional space on this surface. When we look at a landscape in the natural world, our eyes automatically make a judgment and inform our brains that certain things are farther away than other things. Pictorial space attempts to mimic this effect. In a landscape painting, for convenience, we often refer to the *foreground, middle ground,* and *background.* A few paintings actually do show this triple division of planes in space, but in a competent representation of space the various degrees of depth (or distance from the viewer) recede gradually to infinity, with no sharp divisions.

Figure 115 shows a portion of the *Bayeux Tapestry,* an embroidered cloth banner depicting the Norman invasion of England and the events leading up to the Battle of Hastings in 1066. In all, the tapestry is 231 feet (70 meters) long. It shows many different episodes, which are arranged *sequentially,* so that the viewer reads them from left to right like a book. Very little attempt has been made here to create pictorial space. In fact, the space is almost totally flat. Ships in the water seem to be in the same plane as a man sitting on a throne or a knight storming a castle. Rather than being "realistic," the effect is decorative and charming. The *Bayeux Tapestry* also recalls our discussion of time in relation to actual space, since the whole banner cannot possibly be read from any vantage point. The viewer must walk along in front of it, gradually following the episodes.

One simple device prevents the *Bayeux Tapestry* from having absolutely flat pictorial space, and that is the technique of overlapping. Occasionally, as the narrative unfolds, we will come upon a group of figures whose bodies are partially overlapped. Here the designer has made a cautious effort to place one figure behind another, to create pictorial space. For the most part, though, the action remains on the surface.

Denison Cash Stockman has used overlapping in a highly sophisticated manner for his cover design in Figure 116. The vantage point above the crowd adds considerably to the effect of three-dimensional space, as does

115
Harold Swearing Oath, detail of *Bayeux Tapestry.* c. 1073–88. Wool embroidery on linen; height 20″ (51 cm), overall length 231′ (70.4 m). Former Palace of the Bishops, Bayeux.

116
Denison Cash Stockman. Cover design from *Urban Spaces,* by D. K. Specter (New York Graphic Society Books, 1974).

116

the way the figures seem to move across the cover in front of the type, a device that has dramatic impact as well.

Stockman makes use of another device for indicating space by placing his figures in layers or *tiers* of distance. Those at the bottom of the design seem to be directly under us, since we are practically looking at the tops of their heads. As the eye moves toward the upper edge of the composition, the figures move farther away simply because we see them from the side, in greater length. This again is a sophisticated approach involving *foreshortening,* the manner in which objects or planes diminish in length when they are tipped toward the observer.

A more basic use of tiers is found in some of the earliest drawings on record—cave paintings and the paintings and wall carvings of the ancient Egyptians and Mesopotamians. Children have always used this device quite naturally (Fig. 117). Primitive painters even today find tiers a basic tool for depicting distance, as in the painting by Eskimo painter Nauja in Figure 118. The landscape here is divided into well-defined horizontal strips that almost have to be viewed separately. The succession of strips along which the eye must move evokes the feeling of endless space characteristic of the Arctic landscape.

In the arts of the East, the use of layers is more deliberate. There is nothing primitive about the Persian miniature in Figure 119. The figures are beautifully executed, and the many areas of ornamentation are rich in their intricate patterns. The design sense here is sophisticated. If there is no feeling of distance as the Western eye perceives it, the reason lies in the fact that Western conceptions of space are an outgrowth of the Renaissance in fifteenth-century Europe. Prior to that time, European as well as Byzantine, Oriental, and Islamic artists worked from conceptual imagery in which spatial relationships were shown in ways entirely satisfactory to them but different from the perceptual imagery to which the Western world has become accustomed. The Islamic artist who painted the miniature in Figure 119 worked from these older concepts. The paving blocks do not recede into the distance but are vertical, and the rug upon which the upper figures sit is parallel to the picture plane. Still, we know that the lower figures are in front of the Turquoise Palace, while the higher ones sit in a recess within it. The use of tiers tells us exactly what the artist wants us to know about spatial relationships.

117

117
Judy Choate, age 8. *Summer Landscape.*
1978. Felt-tip pen drawing.
Collection of the author.

118
Nauja of Rankin Inlet. Oil painting. 1966.
Hudson's Bay Company Collection,
Winnipeg, Man.

119
Mahmud Muzahib or Follower.
Bahram Gur in the Turquoise Palace on Wednesday, page from the *Khamsa of Nizami.*
16th century. Illuminated manuscript.
Metropolitan Museum of Art, New York
(gift of Alexander Smith Cochran, 1913).

118

119

Nauja's work (Fig. 118) and the *Bayeux Tapestry* (Fig. 115) employ still another means of suggesting distance, *variation in size.* In the portion of the "tapestry" that we show here (it is not really a tapestry, since the designs in tapestry are woven into the fabric and the banner is embroidered), the men in the boat are smaller than those on land, with the waves indicated before the boat also helping to create the appearance of distance. In other parts of the work, men building the boats are as large as the other figures shown on land. In Nauja's painting, the figures on the sled are smaller than the ones before the igloo. The dogs, however, are the same size, and the higher igloo is larger than the lower one. Still, the mountains become lower as they recede toward the top. The very inconsistency of the varying sizes is characteristic of primitive artists, who do not use formulas but who work instinctively to express what they have in mind.

120

Perspective

One of the reasons the devices discussed above are interesting to us is that they are alternatives to *perspective,* the accepted method of Western artists for depicting distance.

In perceptual perspective, which strives for visual reality, there are several possible approaches. One is *aerial* or *atmospheric* perspective. Stated most simply, aerial perspective is based on the fact that objects seen from a distance seem less clear, their colors more muted than objects that are close. This effect is caused by two factors: the softening quality of the air between the viewer and the subject, and the inability of the human eye to distinguish clearly forms and colors at a distance. Aerial perspective tries to duplicate this reality by a progressive graying and blurring as the composition goes back into space.

The most painstaking and self-conscious search for "true" representation of space on a flat surface took place during the Renaissance. Artists of the fourteenth century had attempted to place their figures in a shallow space, frequently in little buildings, to create an architectural setting (Fig. 120). The progression into space ends right behind the figures, and the result often looks like a stage set.

By the fifteenth century artists had formulated the principles of *linear perspective* into an exact science. As practiced then, it is extremely complicated, but the basic assumptions are simple. First, as had long been realized, objects in the distance appear to be smaller than those close to the viewer. Second, parallel lines or planes receding into the distance seem to meet at some point, which is known as the *vanishing point.* We have all noticed this phenomenon in rows of telephone poles or in looking down an expanse of railroad track, for instance. The Renaissance painters sharpened their mastery of linear perspective by actually constructing lines and vanishing points in their pictures. In theory, once the lines were removed, we would have the same visual experience in looking at the painting as in viewing the actual scene (Figs. 121, 122).

120
Giotto. *Annunciation to Anna.* c. 1305–10. Fresco. Arena Chapel, Padua.

121
Piero della Francesca and Luciano Laurana. *View of an Ideal City* (detail). c. 1460. Tempera on panel, 1'11" × 6'6¾" (.58 × 2 m). Galleria Nazionale delle Marche, Palazzo Ducale, Urbino.

122
Perspective drawing based on *View of an Ideal City.*

123
Auguste Renoir. *La Première Sortie* (The First Outing). c. 1875–76. Oil on canvas, 25½ × 19¾" (65 × 50 cm). The National Gallery, London.

121

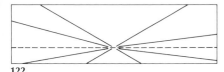

122

123

Implied Space

Until the late nineteenth century, paintings were composed within the four edges of a canvas. In figure compositions, the figures were usually grouped toward the center of the composition in order to draw the eye toward a focal point, and frequently the lines of the architecture and furnishings and even of the figures themselves would be carefully planned to lead toward the predominant character.

The nineteenth-century Impressionist painters broke with tradition in many ways. Most notable was their use of color to imply the diffraction of light (see p. 100). Equally unconventional was their interpretation of space. In paintings like the one by Renoir in Figure 123, the action is not contained within four margins. Instead, the composition is a vignette of a world that flows beyond, a part of the larger space that is *implied*. Our

Peter Voulkos

Bronze Sculpture

124

124
Harry Murphy. Catalog cover for
Peter Voulkos Sculpture Exhibition at the
San Francisco Museum of Modern Art. 1973.
Printed graphics, 10 × 10″ (25.4 × 25.4 cm).

125
Victor Vasarely. *Sir-Ris.* 1952—62.
Oil on canvas, 6′6″ × 3′3″ (1.98 × .99 m).
Courtesy Vasarely Center, New York.

attention is focused on a central character, to be sure, but she is watching
something we cannot see, and she thus becomes a part of the greater
audience. It is interesting to note that Renoir has utilized his knowledge of
perception to indicate this audience. The young lady with her violets is in
focus, but the other figures are intentionally blurred, as they would naturally be when our eye is focused on the foreground.

Graphic artists find the device of implied space an effective kind of
symbolism, a means of suggesting much by simple means. In the museum
catalog cover in Figure 124 we are tantalized by the fact that we are being
shown only *part* of a form since the sculpture recedes beyond the confines
of the border. Instinctively we want to know how far the form goes and

what its total shape must be. A complete work could have made an effective image, but by cutting it off at the edge of the catalog, the designer arouses our curiosity. At the same time, he lets us know that there is much more to be seen, in fact, a whole exhibit of interesting works.

The optical or "Op" artists of the mid-twentieth century investigated spatial perceptions of a different sort. Through careful manipulation of lines and shapes, the Op artist creates the impression of bulges, undulations, or actual movement in space (Fig. 125). This type of visual illusion is purely sensory. It relates to the *optical* reaction of the human eye to light and color.

125

126

127

Light and Tonality in Depicting Space

126
Jean Baptiste Corot.
Woman Gathering Faggots. 28⅜ × 22½"
(72.14 × 57.15 cm). Metropolitan Museum
of Art, The Mr. and Mrs. Isaac D. Fletcher
Collection (bequest of Isaac D. Fletcher,
1917).

127
Alexander Calder. *Red Petals.* 1942.
Mobile-stabile. Painted iron and
aluminum; height 8'6" (2.59 m).
Collection of The Arts Club of Chicago.

In mentioning aerial perspective, we noted that space or distance is depicted by a softening of color as objects recede. The softening is actually a lightening of color, as well as a graying of *tone*. This quality of lightness or darkness, of brightness or grayness, is referred to as *tonality*. It is perhaps most obvious in looking at a painting that has been reproduced in black-and-white. In the work in Figure 126 the foreground is dark, with highlights striking the figure and bringing out the detail in the bark and leaves of the surrounding trees. This area is almost silhouetted against the middle ground, which appears to be flooded with light. The few trees visible in this section have little detail. Beyond is a hill that is simply a grayed form. We know by its contour that it is covered with trees, but we see no individual trunks. Tonality combines with loss of detail to suggest that this landscape stretches away into the distance.

Space can be depicted in an opposite way as well, by highlighting a center of interest and implying receding distance by surrounding areas of darkness. Rembrandt made this technique an effective means of expressing religious symbolism. In Plate 5 (p. 54) the central figures are bathed in a mystical glow while the less important figures blend into a background rich with dark color. Here great distance is not important, yet the dramatic lighting establishes a feeling of space, not only behind the figures but also above them, where the arms of the cross are barely discernible.

Light is used in many other ways. The Dutch painters flooded rooms with sunlight, giving a feeling of large airy spaces; religious painters have used beams of light to give a sense of drama; and landscape painters have worked for striking effects of light on water and on snow. We will see in Chapter 7 that there can be no color without light, but in becoming aware of the importance of space, we must realize that the depiction of space, distance, and form all depend on light as well.

Space, Motion, and Time

Space inevitably implies motion, which involves time. Meteors and satellites move through space and so do people and animals. Leaves fall, plants thrust upward, and fog drifts in response to the motion of air currents. When a painter uses tonality to depict distance there is the implication of movement—of light rays, of air, and of the human eye. When the viewer responds, not only does it require time to become aware of the illusion, but the movement and tonality within the work also indicate the passage of time, if only momentarily.

Three-dimensional design is even more obviously involved with motion and time. Any building is useless unless people move through it. Contemporary architects design buildings so indoor space and outdoor space flow back and forth, integrating the structure with its environment.

We mentioned on page 72 that sculptures of architectural scale are meant to be walked around and through and even climbed upon. Many sculptures move as well. The principle of the mobile is a careful balance of parts to facilitate continuous movement (Fig. 127). Light sculpture such as the one in Figure 60 relies heavily on movement for its effectiveness; in fact, its title includes the word *ballet.*

Light, motion, and time are among the most dynamic of the materials of the designer, materials that we will discover repeatedly in our exploration of design. They can be considered as three aspects of the enormous subject of space, a field we have only touched upon in this discussion.

6 Texture

Texture involves the tactile sense, or sense of touch. As infants, we touch before we see, and through the years the role of texture in our lives remains a vital one. Although in general a totally smooth environment could seem sterile and a totally rough one menacing, people react to textures in different ways. The variety of texture in our environment accounts for much of its interest and livability.

Texture and pattern are inevitably intertwined. A pine cone has a distinct pattern and also has a texture that feels rough to the hand. A patterned fabric gives us a *visual* sense of texture, making us feel surface variations even when none exist to the touch. An *area* of texture becomes pattern. In a design sense, pattern is created when a unit is repeated (Fig. 128). A unit thus repeated as a thematic element becomes a *motif*.

Since a strong psychological element is involved in texture and we can feel surface variations even when our eyes perceive a smooth surface, we make a distinction between *tactile* and *visual* textures. Actual changes in plane that can be felt by the fingers result in tactile textures, whereas variations in light and dark on smooth *or* unsmooth surfaces produce visual textures. A chunk of porous lava rock has definite tactile texture; if we pass our fingers over it, we can feel bumps and hollows. A smooth granite pebble also has texture, but it is visual texture resulting from flecks in the composition of the stone. Similarly, a glaze on pottery may be smooth to the touch yet be textured to the eye by fragments of chemical oxides suspended in the glaze (Fig. 129).

128

128
Tapis (ceremonial skirt), c. 1900–1925. Lampong District, Sumatra, Indonesia. Silk and cotton ground with couched metallic embroidery, 46 × 49½″ (1.17 × 1.26 m). Atlantic Richfield Company Corporate Collection.

129
Kim Bruce. *Tea Set.* 1975. Stoneware. Courtesy the artist.

130
Two extremes of texture—smooth and rough.

Texture

Textures are so much a part of our environment that we generally take them for granted. The two kinds of tactile textures, rough and smooth, in Figure 130 are good examples of textures we see every day but seldom notice. The clothes we wear, the homes in which we live, and the world in which we move are all a vast collection of textures. From the rough bark of the trunk to the smooth texture of new leaves, a single tree may exhibit several different textures. The textures of different foods add immensely to the pleasure of eating, and good cooks make use of that fact, adding crisp croutons to soups and salads, smooth sauces to fibrous vegetables, and crunchy nuts as toppings for desserts.

129

130

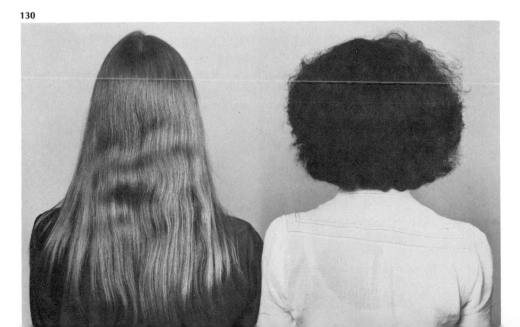

131

Cesar (Cesar Baldaccini).
The Yellow Buick. 1961. Compressed
automobile, 4′11½″ × 2′6¾″ × 2⅞″
(1.51 × .78 × .8 m). Museum of Modern Art,
New York (gift of Mr. and Mrs. John Rewald).

132

Nobuo Sekine. *Phases of Nothingness—Cone.*
1972. Black granite, height 11¾″ (30 cm).
Courtesy Tokyo Gallery.

133

Philip Cornelius. Covered jar. 1981.
Charcoal-glazed stoneware, height 12″
(30.48 cm). Courtesy Marcia Rodell Gallery,
Los Angeles.

134

Inca feather tunic from Peru. 1100–1400.
Feathers knotted on cords stitched to
plain weave cotton ground 5′11″ × 2′9″
(1.81 × .84 m). Los Angeles County
Museum of Art (gift of Mr. and Mrs.
William T. Sesnon, Jr., 1974).

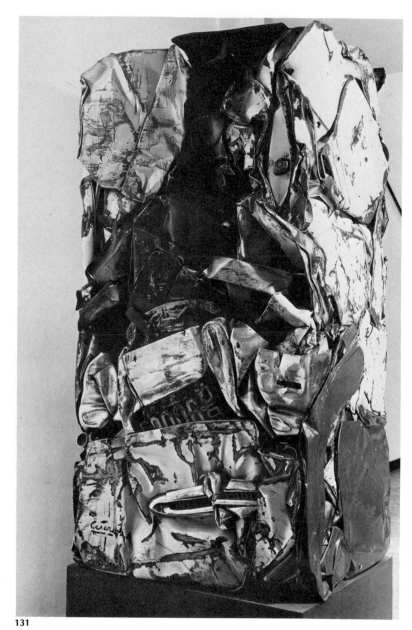

131

An extreme of *tactile texture* is illustrated in Figure 131. This work, which is actually an automobile compressed into a cube, has deep indentations all over its surface. It is easy to imagine how it would feel to run our hands over such a piece. However, this strong tactile texture translates visually as well, with the deep shadows within the crevices creating a powerful visual texture.

The works of Japanese sculptor Nobuo Sekine provide beautiful examples of textural *contrast.* In *Phases of Nothingness* in Figure 132, the artist has juxtaposed the perfectly smooth cone of black granite against a rough base suggestive of rock. The two sections blend and yet each acquires greater interest in contrast to the other.

One of the reasons handcrafted objects are treasured is the variety and warmth of their texture. The stoneware jar in Figure 133 has an individual quality that could not be duplicated. Its charm is partly the result of the material, but even more it is the result of the way in which the hands of the potter have worked. In addition, the glaze reminds us of geological formations after long weathering, and we feel the affinity of clay to the other materials of the earth.

Fabrics offer some of the richest textures in everyday life and assume their own symbolism. Smooth satins and lush velvets connote elegance, whereas nubby woolens make us think of the outdoors and the active life. The Incas of pre-Columbian Peru wove entire garments from feathers for an unusually lush texture (Fig. 134). Feathers were carefully sorted by color to display distinct hues as well as to show fine gradations of color.

Textures are of particular importance in interior design, since variations in texture have much to do with physical and emotional comfort. Generally speaking, smooth textures in an interior can seem cold, and when they predominate, the atmosphere may actually feel chilly. Rough textures, on the other hand, have a warmth about them that makes most people feel at ease—the kinds of textures found in brick and stone, uneven wall sur-

132

134

133

135

faces, and in thick carpets and nubby draperies. The rooms in Figures 135 and 136 show extremes of textural treatment. In the first room everything is smooth. In the second, what could be a bare loftlike room has been made warm and personal almost entirely by the tactile textures of the brick wall, rattan chairs, and plants, and the visual textures of bare wood and textiles, brought to a focal point in a striking painting. The variety of texture is as important as any specific texture, for the environment is enhanced by the changing sensations offered to the eye and hand.

For centuries artists have depicted textures on the flat surface of canvas, but texture in painting can also be real. Certain artists, including Vincent van Gogh, developed a technique of laying oil paint on canvas in a thick, pastelike *impasto* (Fig. 137). This effect increases the illusion of reality on the flat canvas but, perhaps more important, it also lends an energetic physical texture to the work.

In this century, artists have added texture to their paintings by introducing diverse materials (Fig. 138). The Cubists, whose style is characterized by the reduction of shapes and forms to simple overlapping planes, sometimes employed actual objects for texture. Georges Braque pasted bits of newspaper and other materials onto the canvas and then integrated them with the painted portions. This type of composition is known as *collage*, from the French word for pasting. Later artists incorporated three-dimensional objects into their work, thus obscuring the dividing line between painting and sculpture. Such works are often referred to as *constructions*, and they represent the textural element carried to the extreme.

135
A ''Minimal'' all-white living room designed by Bill Ehrlich is nearly all smooth in texture except for one visual accent.

136
Hugh Hardy, designer. Both visual and tactile textures contribute to a feeling of warmth and informality in this New York City living room.

137
Vincent van Gogh. *Cypresses* (detail). 1889. Oil on canvas, 36¾ × 29⅛" (1.01 × .74 m). Metropolitan Museum of Art, New York (Rogers Fund, 1949).

138
Romare Bearden. *Carolina Shout,* from ''Of the Blues'' series. 1974. Collage with acrylic and lacquer, 37½ × 51" (.93 × 1.28 m). Mint Museum, Charlotte, N.C. (funds provided by National Endowment for the Arts and the Charlotte Debutante Club).

136

137

138

The two fabrics shown in Figures 139 and 140 illustrate the difference between tactile and *visual textures.* The tapestry from Quebec is immensely varied in surface interest, yet there is no contrast in color and all the shapes are based on the rectangle. The entire composition is a study in tactile texture. The batik in Figure 140, on the other hand, is done on smooth cotton. The tremendous interest of the piece comes from the diverse shapes and the lively visual texture of light against dark, and from the veined quality that is characteristic of *batik,* a dying process in which wax is used to block out portions of the fabric.

Visual texture has always been a predominant feature of two-dimensional design. The dense concentration of black characters on white makes the Chinese scroll in Figure 141 rich in texture. The clump of bamboo adds a dramatic texture of its own, its thick leaves balancing the delicate spacing between the calligraphic characters that form the larger portion of the composition.

139

139
Helena Barynina. Tapestry, woven cotton, flax, and plastic. Province of Quebec.

140
Detail of cotton batik by Nimba tribeswomen, Liberia.

141
Li Shan (1711–? [after 1754]).
Bamboo and Calligraphy. Hanging scroll, ink on paper; 4'4" × 2'5¼" (1.32 × .74 m). Collection John M. Crawford, Jr., New York.

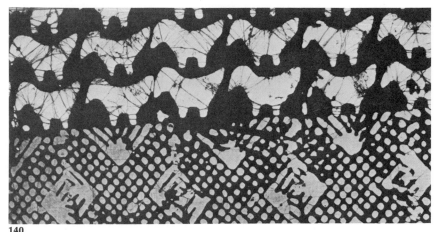

140
141

一萬一萬臺一部出原二種武夷賽骨一葉二臻臺一葉兩師金佰嫦娥窟
無懷則偕此諸千古敢同孔子謂濱載送老漁午某皇祐盍嫣
孔血祖龍惡碧山江至于寺荒武堂崖還誰懷抱碧狠拜千圍鶴民冲天鼠東坡祐木
風首當與可嫌楨萬上長梅茂嚴呂何清揚天水夫人為清隆翠篠娟風露香
青藤授蹤惟清淮云竹祖孫不見畫家法肯構堂湘南照南昭
郝窩八老諸懷人掌竹破吾鄉馬之鼎不與
且園青且園怪鼎以瓢此刀切玉
蟲蝕斥老夫寫竹又一家枯藤百丈
沿穰蛇鳥篆青魚相盤好手啥乎
昨日慣有喧龍手轉眼掛雲
頤白生霜華馬鳥不至
尾崔辭鸚哥毛黑豈逢
鴝菖葉二胡益卯
乾隆十四年九月
疫堂順民人李鱔

142

Similarly, the chalk drawing in Figure 142 presents such a rich, velvety visual texture that the sensory experience is almost tactile. It is interesting that the areas of darkness do not have the same textural quality as the lighter portions. The same subtle use of light and dark that has modeled the figure into the appearance of three dimensions has provided the textural surface of the drawing.

Texture Through Light

Both tactile and visual textures are dependent upon light. The Greeks developed this knowledge into a high skill, enriching their temples with carefully designed borders and molding so the brilliant sunlight would cause a texture of light and shadow (Fig. 143).

The architects of the Middle Ages used light in a dramatic way by installing magnificent stained-glass windows, whose many-colored panes poured a mosaic of light into the vast interiors of cathedrals. The light emphasized the tactile textures of stone, tapestries, and wood carving and created as well a visual texture of color.

A twentieth-century adaptation of these techniques was used by Le Corbusier when he designed his chapel of Notre-Dame-du-Haut at Ronchamp (Fig. 144). Both exterior and interior walls are rich in tactile texture, but even more interesting is the visual texture provided by the light admitted through windows of varying size, shape, and placement. The windows themselves add texture to the walls, and throughout the day, as the sun moves, the light coming through them textures the entire interior. Some of the windows are painted with scattered designs and inscriptions in red and blue, hinting at the effect of stained glass.

142
Pierre Paul Prud'hon. *La Source.* c. 1801. Black and white chalk on blue-gray paper, 21³/₁₆ × 15⁵/₁₆″ (54 × 39 cm). Sterling and Francine Clark Art Institute, Williamstown, Mass.

143
Triglyphs and metope on the Parthenon, Athens. 448–432 B.C. Metope, 4′8″ × 4′2″ (1.42 × 1.27 m).

144
Le Corbusier. *Notre-Dame-du-Haut.* 1950–55. Interior view of the south wall. Ronchamp, France.

143
144

145

145
Alexander Liberman. *Sabine Women II.*
1981. Painted steel, 8'6" × 10' × 11'
(2.59 × 3.05 × 3.35 m). Courtesy
André Emmerich Gallery, New York.

146
Detail drawing of Ahir skirt. Embroidered
cotton, mirrors; 33" (83.3 cm). Kutch
region of India. UCLA Museum of Cultural
History, Los Angeles.

147
Ahir skirt. Embroidered cotton, mirrors;
33" (83.3 cm). Kutch region of India.
Gift of William Lloyd Davis and Mr. and
Mrs. Richard B. Rogers.

Light molds the forms of realistic sculpture, providing shading similar to what we have seen in the drawing in Figure 142. In Alexander Liberman's *Sabine Women II* (Fig. 145), however, it performs a different function. This work is composed of bands and shapes of steel painted and interlaced to create a sense of the chaos that must have prevailed when Roman soldiers carried off the women of the Sabines, a colony in northeast Italy conquered by the Romans. Light weaves among the layers of steel, highlighting and casting shadows. The result is one of tremendous activity. The work does not have texture; it *is* texture. We are not aware of individual surfaces or of surface quality generally but of a mass of churning texture.

Pattern

We implied earlier that the difference between texture and pattern is one of degree. A single brick is textured, but a wall of textured bricks creates a pattern. If texture and pattern are not synonymous, there is certainly considerable overlapping. Any pattern has visual texture but not all texture embodies a pattern. The Liberian batik in Figure 140 is patterned, and the windows of Notre-Dame-du-Haut (Fig. 144) form both a patterned wall and a pattern of light within the interior. For purposes of differentiation, we will assume that pattern is an extension of texture.

Pattern as Repetition of Design

The design motif in Figure 146 has been embroidered by Ahir women in northern India and displays diverse shapes and symbols. Alone it makes an interesting design. When it is repeated around the border of a skirt, however, it becomes an entirely different entity, a border pattern (Fig. 147).

146

147

148

149

148
Packages for automotive and brake products for Wagner Division of McGraw Edison. Red and blue on a white background; measurements vary. Design: Ko Noda.

149
Shuji Asada. *Form-B.* 1980. Stencil dying (cotton), 7'2½" × 7'2½" (2.2 × 2.2 m).

150
Jane Hamilton-Merritt. *Norway Street.* 1976. Photograph.

151
Constantino Nivola. Mural façade of Covenant Mutual Insurance Building, Hartford, Conn. 1958. Sand-cast concrete relief, 30 × 110' (9.14 × 33.53 m).

It is the repetitive quality of pattern that makes it distinctive; in an allover design no single feature predominates. Pattern lends itself well to backgrounds—wallpaper, carpets, and fabrics. Pattern is a feature of gift-wrapping paper and can be effective in package design. Using simply the name of a product in type that has been carefully chosen and placed, a pattern can fulfill two requirements of package design: improving the appearance of the merchandise and impressing the name of the product on the mind of the buyer (Fig. 148).

An allover pattern gains interest when the motif is varied. In Figure 149 a strong geometric unit is placed at 90-degree angles, going clockwise. There is a basic consistency of pattern but there is also a vitality in its conception that prevents the allover pattern from being monotonous.

Pattern as Surface Design

A surface can be patterned without the use of repetition. Many of the streets in Europe are patterned with cobblestones, carefully chosen as to size, shape, and color, to produce intriguing patterns (Fig. 150). Drainage gulleys may be outlined in one size and shape of stone, and sewer covers lie like the center of a flower in a radiating pattern. The basic units, the stones, are similar, it is true, yet they do not constitute a deliberate motif. Rather, they form a texture that translates into the larger areas of pattern.

Although twentieth-century cities seldom put such decorative efforts into their busy thoroughfares, texture and pattern are used to relieve the stark walls of concrete and glass buildings. In Figure 151, panels of relief sculpture (sculpture that is attached to a background) have been cast by pouring wet concrete into molds formed of sand. The play of light over the textured surface, casting accents of shadow, suggests a relationship to the natural environment that is more pleasing than would be the sterility of cold, smooth walls.

150

151

Interacting Patterns

Frequently there is an element of surprise in pattern. Units placed in repetition or in combination with other units over a large area inevitably create new units that even the designer may not have foreseen. Often these are the result of *negative space,* the space *around* the designed units, or playing *through* them. The wrought-iron screen in Figure 152 is composed of identical units fastened on vertical iron poles. The shapes themselves are interesting. However, within the allover pattern, new shapes become apparent, between the units, and flow through into ovoid shapes that change with the viewpoint. Seen as it is in the illustration, against white paper, the pattern seems almost dominated by the light shapes, in other words, the spaces.

The pattern on the Ahir skirt (Fig. 147) is quite different from the motif that composes it, for the motif is placed continuously to form a flowing band. Similarly, in Figure 149 there are diagonals that carry from square to square, creating a new design different from elements within any separate square. In designing an allover pattern, the artist is in fact making two designs: the individual motif, and the design that results when the motif is repeated. Often the placement of the motifs in relation to one another is a major decision of the designer. Any of the allover patterns shown would change character if the motifs were placed at different angles or different distances from one another; thus texture and pattern become two aspects of a single design element.

152

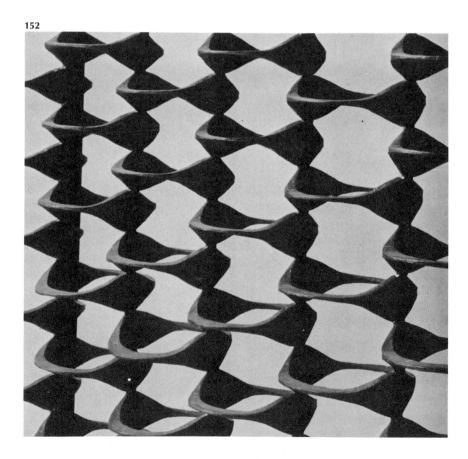

152
Wrought-iron lattice.
Werkkunstschule, Aachen, Germany.

7 Color

Of all the design elements, color undoubtedly awakens the greatest emotional response. Although it is not necessary for the creation of a great work of art, it suggests a mood and depth of experience that cannot be achieved in any other way. We speak of the color wheel in the visual arts in much the way that we speak of the tonal scale in music. Like the basic notes of the musical scale that can be expanded into symphonies, colors can be combined in an unlimited number of ways and have an enormous capacity to manipulate our emotions. Undoubtedly, color is one of the most powerful tools of the designer.

Color is both an art and a science. Physicists explain the abstract theories of color and its relationship to light, as well as the optical principles involved in color sensation. Chemists formulate rules for mixing and applying colors. Psychologists study emotional responses to specific colors. The artist needs to understand all these factors before developing a personal color system and symbolism by which color will fulfill an individual aesthetic purpose.

Color and Light

Without light there can be no color. Things that we identify as being red, green, or orange are not innately those colors, but we perceive them as such because of the action of light upon their surface.

What we call light represents only a small portion of the electromagnetic field, the part that is visible (Fig. 153). Within that portion, variations in the wavelengths of the vibrations cause the viewer to see different colors. The longest wavelength is perceived as red, the shortest as violet or purple.

Although ancient Greek philosophers asserted that color is a matter of perception rather than a physical property, it was not until 1666 that Isaac Newton established the relationship between color and sunlight. As an experiment, he directed a beam of sunlight into a glass prism. Since glass is denser than air, the light was refracted, or bent, as it passed through. Newton expected this, but he did not expect the light to be dispersed into

153

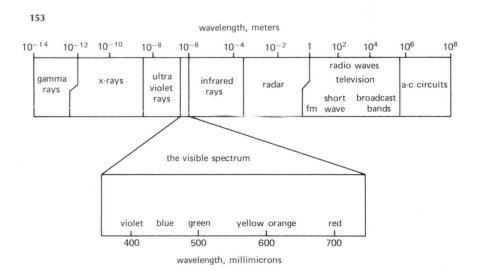

153
This diagram of the electromagnetic field shows the portion of the spectrum that is visible to the human eye—in other words, what we call "light." A millicron is one thousandth of a micron which, in turn, is one millionth of a meter.

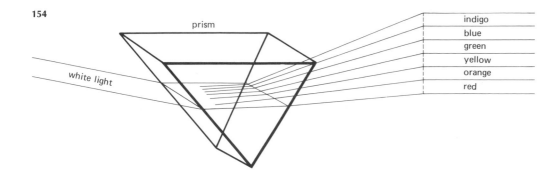

prism

white light

indigo
blue
green
yellow
orange
red

colors as it left the prism. The short waves in the light were refracted more and the long waves less, and as they emerged from the prism they arranged themselves systematically into the colors of the rainbow: indigo, blue, green, yellow, orange, and red (Fig. 154). There is no purple in the natural spectrum of color, but where the first and last colors, red and indigo, combine or overlap, the result is purple or violet. This fact gave Newton the idea of joining the colors into a circle or color wheel so the flow from tone to tone would be continuous. After separating sunlight into its color components with the first prism, he used a second prism to reverse the action, combining the colors back into sunlight. This established the fact that color is basically white light and further, that *in light,* all colors mixed together result in white.

The mechanism by which surfaces produce color is not thoroughly understood, but it apparently is related to the molecular structure of the surface, as inorganic compounds are generally colorless in solution and the hue of organic compounds can be changed by altering them chemically. Most colors seen in everyday life are caused by the partial absorption of white light. A surface that we call red will absorb all the rays *except* those from the wavelength that produces red, so we perceive red. When light is totally absorbed by a surface, the result is black. Many factors influence the way in which light is absorbed or reflected. The colors in a raindrop or a soap bubble are caused by *diffraction,* the phenomenon in which a wave of light, after passing the edge of a solid or opaque object, spreads out instead of continuing in a straight line. The blue of the sky is the result of the scattering of short-wavelength blue components of sunlight by tiny particles suspended in the atmosphere. A tree in the sunlight will seem one color on its shaded side and another on its side in the direct light, and its leaves can show tremendous variation in color, depending upon the way the light strikes them. The Impressionist painters of the later nineteenth century exploited this phenomenon to a high degree.

Impressionism sought to divorce art from intellectual interpretations, to paint what we actually see rather than what we *think* we see. If we know a house to be red, we may be tempted to paint it the same red all over, when in fact the light striking it would produce many different reds and other colors as well. The Impressionists, then, tried to see forms in terms of shimmering light and color, breaking up visual images into tiny dabs of colored paint (Pl. 6, p. 103). They abandoned hard edges and lines, because they felt that these do not really exist in nature but are supplied by our reasoning process. The aim was to bypass our thought processes, to translate visual impressions directly into sensory experience.

154
A ray of white light projected through a prism separates into the hues of the rainbow.

Perception of Color

The Greek philosophers assumed that color was not a quality of the object but a product of the mind that interprets the image striking the retina. Since the nineteenth century it has been apparent that the retina of the eye does not record each variation or even every shade of color that comes within its range. Instead, it limits itself to a few basic colors from which all the others are derived. This means that the photochemical processes of vision are selective, allowing us on the level of conscious perception to see colors as variations and combinations of the few that register on the retina. The discovery that the perception of the object differs from the object itself laid the foundation for the concept of modern art. A close look at Pissarro's painting in Plate 6 makes it clear that the artist was not painting grass or trees or a human figure realistically. He simply applied brushstrokes to the canvas in such a way that we could interpret them to be objects within our experience. The grass is not an ordinary expanse of green but a rich texture of small strokes of yellow and blue and, when they overlap, of green. If they did not overlap in a physical or *partitive* mixture, the eye would perceive an average of the wavelengths of the two colors, in other words, gray. The result of the intermixture is vibrant and alive, but it is our perception that tells us it is green and our intelligence that makes us know that it is grass.

There are numerous theories of color perception, many of which are highly technical. Of more immediate importance to us are the experiments that successful artists have made in the field of color perception. The Op (optical) painters are of particular interest. Although they did not always work in color (Figs. 67, p. 43, and 125, p. 81), their experiments have had a major impact on both painting and design.

Victor Vasarely carried out extensive experimentation in color, exploring its *architectonic* (structural) qualities, its possibilities for three-dimensional illusion, and its interrelationships through gradations of tone. His work in Plate 7 (p. 103) is based on red, blue, and yellow as is Pissarro's composition in Plate 6. By grading the colors from light to dark in squares and circles, however, Vasarely has revealed possibilities far beyond those usually associated with these three colors: a vibration emanates from the juxtaposition of variations of color, and the sense of depth fluctuates as we gaze at the surface of the painting. Each unit influences its surroundings in such a way that the shapes become reflectors and vibrators, each one changing and moving as a result of the others. One senses that the artist must have worked in a state of both curiosity and excitement, for it seems unlikely that such vibrancy could be the result of careful planning.

Color Theory

From the tremendous field of color experimentation, certain theories have evolved concerning the origins of colors and their interaction. Most of these are based on the color wheel and on a group of specific basic or *primary* colors from which all other colors can be mixed.

For many years, students learned color theory on the basis of studies begun in the eighteenth century and culminating in the work of Herbert E. Ives. Ives devised a color wheel based on red, yellow, and blue as the

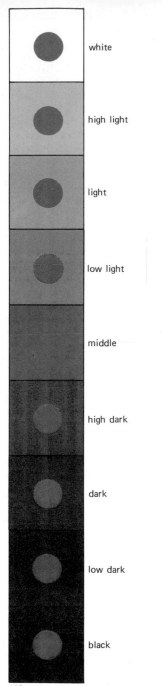

white

high light

light

low light

middle

high dark

dark

low dark

black

156

155

Munsell arranged the hues around a central pole that represents value gradations of gray from white to black. Each hue on the circular band is designated by a letter, such as *R* for red, which then flows through the entire spectrum until it returns to *R-P* for red-purple, and so back to red. The radiating horizontal bars represent numerically designated gradations of each hue from gray, at the central pole, to highest intensity at the outer end of the bar. If a hue extends beyond the circle it is because of unusually strong intensity.

156

The gray scale.

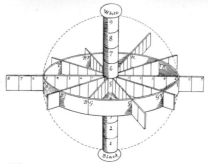

155

primary colors (Pl. 8, p. 104). By mixing any two primaries together, one obtains a *secondary* color: green from yellow and blue, orange from yellow and red, violet from blue and red. Going a step further, one can mix a primary and a secondary color to produce a third group, known as *tertiary* colors: yellow-orange, orange-red, red-violet, violet-blue, blue-green, and yellow-green. When all of these colors are placed in such a way that they seem to flow naturally, or to *modulate,* into one another, the basic color wheel results.

Any color wheel is to some extent arbitrary. Ives designed another wheel for use in mixing dyes and pigments, and physicists who work with light use still another. There are wheels that concern themselves with human vision and the sequence in which we see colors. Wheels vary in number of colors shown from eight to a hundred or more. They also vary in the names given the same color. What Ives calls orange, Albert H. Munsell calls yellow-red, and Ives' violet becomes purple in Munsell's designation. Such variation is not limited to color theorists, of course. Anyone who reads newspaper and magazine advertising is exposed to originality in color naming carried to the extreme. In an effort at enticing associations, firms offer plum sofas or melon-colored coats, leaving the reader to puzzle over which variety of plum or melon is being referred to.

In the hope of avoiding confusion, we will limit our discussion to the most scientific of the color systems, the one devised in 1912 by Albert Munsell. In this system, color is described in terms of three attributes: *hue, value,* and *chroma* (or intensity). There are five key hues: red, yellow, green, blue, and purple (Pl. 9, p. 104). Secondary hues thus become yellow-red, green-yellow, blue-green, purple-blue, and red-purple. Munsell used a numerical scale to designate variations in *value* or lightness, and *intensity* or brightness, of hues so any given color could be defined with precision. For this reason the Munsell system has become a standard method of designating color for government agencies such as the National Bureau of Standards, as well as for systems of standards in Japan, Great Britain, and Germany.

Color Properties

The spherical diagram in Figure 155 demonstrates visually the three properties of color, as Munsell understood them, and their interrelationships. Here color is arranged in three scales: a circular scale of hues, a vertical scale of values, and a horizontal scale of intensity, or chroma. *Hue* is the name by which we identify a color. It refers to the pure state of the color, unmixed and unmodified. The hue red means pure red with no white, black, or other colors added. Hue is the basis for the other color properties.

Value refers to the relative lightness or darkness of a color. It can best be understood by a study of the *gray scale* (Fig. 156). We show the scale with

Plate 6
Camille Pissarro.
Woman in a Field.
1887. Oil on canvas,
21 × 25½" (54 × 65 cm).
Louvre, Paris.

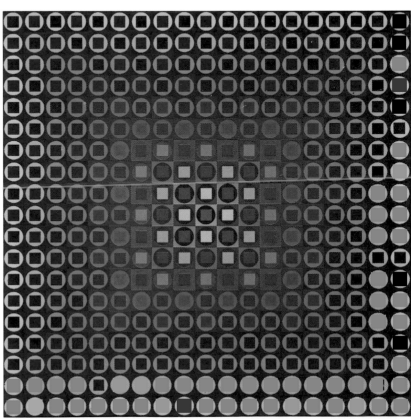

Plate 7
Victor Vasarely. *KEZDI-III*. 1966. 33 × 33"
(84 × 84 cm).

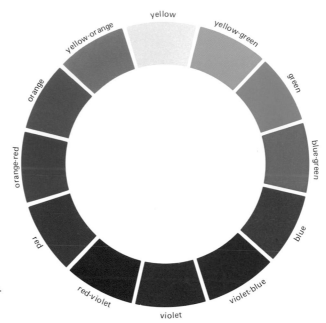

Plate 8
The traditional color wheel by Herbert Ives begins with primary colors of red, yellow, and blue. From these three hues are formed the secondary colors, orange, green, and violet. Tertiary colors result from combining a primary with a secondary.

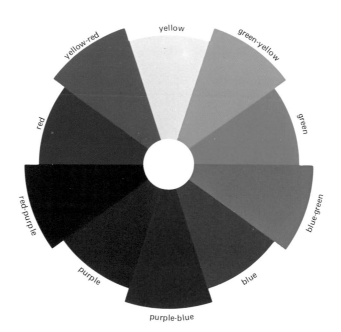

Plate 9
The Munsell color wheel is based on five key hues: red, yellow, blue, green, and purple. From these primaries are formed secondaries of yellow-red, green-yellow, blue-green, purple-blue, and red-purple. Although the terminology differs slightly and the Munsell wheel has ten colors to Ives's twelve, the colors themselves are essentially the same.

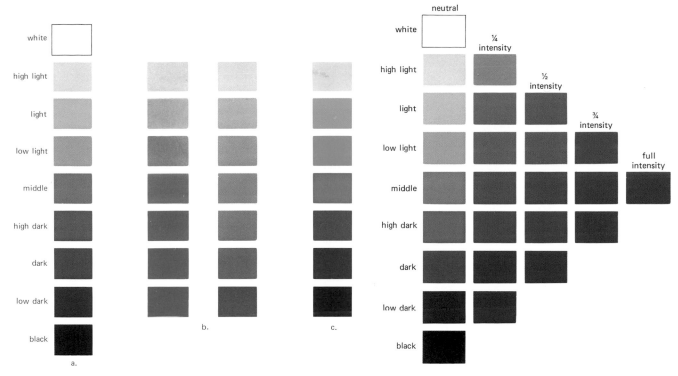

white

high light

light

low light

middle

high dark

dark

low dark

black

a.

b.

c.

neutral

white

¼ intensity

high light

½ intensity

light

¾ intensity

low light

full intensity

middle

high dark

dark

low dark

black

Plate 10

The value scale indicates shades of gray between pure white and absolute black (a). Hues in the color wheel can also be arranged in such a value scale, as with yellow-red and blue (b). At normal value, all the hues forming the color wheel can also be arranged in a vertical scale of lightness and darkness, with gradations from yellow to purple or violet (c).

Plate 11

The intensity or chroma scale shows the full range of brightness of which a hue is capable; from pure color at full intensity to the varied tones made possible by successive degrees of graying.

Plate 12a

According to the additive principle in light, the three primary colors, red, blue, and green, when overlapped, create the secondary colors of yellow, cyan, and magenta. When combined, they add up to white light.

Plate 12b

In the subtractive principle, the process is reversed. Yellow, cyan, and magenta are considered the primary colors and when they are overlapped, they produce red, blue, and green. When combined, they add up to black.

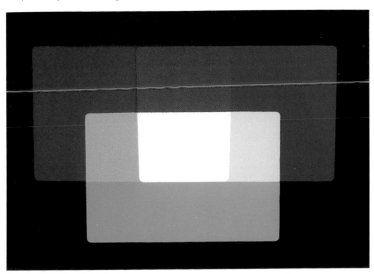

Plate 13
Experiment in *after-image.* If you stare
at the red circle for half a minute, then
switch to the white one, you will see not
white but blue-green, the complement of
red.

Plate 14
Experiment in *reversed after-image.* Stare
at the yellow circles for half a minute,
then switch to the white square below the
circles. You will see not circles but the
curved diamond shapes between circles and
squares, and they will be not white but
yellow.

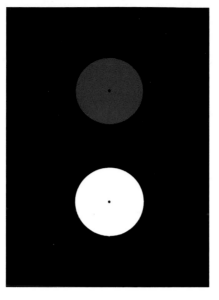
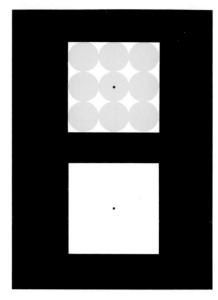

Plate 15
Albert Bierstadt. *Rocky Mountains.* 1863. 6'1¼" × 10'¾" (1.86 × 3.07 m).
Metropolitan Museum of Art, Rogers Fund, 1907.

Plate 16
Barbara Chase-Riboud. *The Cape.* 1973. Multicolored bronze, hemp, and copper;
8'1½" × 4'10½" × 4'10½". (2.48 × 1.49 × 1.49 m). The Lannan Foundation, Palm Springs, Florida.

Plate 17
Page from the beginning of the Christmas story in St. Matthew. *Lindesfarne Gospels*. Folio 29.
Late 7th century. Courtesy Trustees of the British Museum.

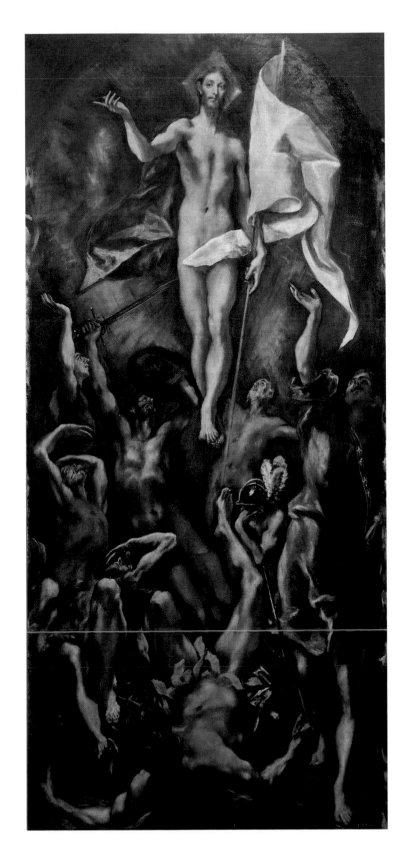

Plate 18
El Greco. *The Resurrection of Christ.* 1600–1605.
Oil on canvas, 9′1¼″ × 4′5″ (2.75 × 1.35 m).
Prado, Madrid.

Plate 19
Barnett Newman. *Dionysius*. 1949. Oil on canvas, 5'9" × 4' (1.75 × 1.21 m). Collection Annalee Newman, New York.

157

157
Albert Gleizes. *Port.* 1912. Pencil, 6 × 7⅝"
(15.24 × 19.3 cm). The Solomon R.
Guggenheim Museum, New York.

a center circle of the same middle value in each of nine blocks ranging
from white to black. Compare the changes in the circles and squares in
Vasarely's work in Plate 7 (p. 103). In both cases, the changes are the result
of the background or adjacent value. The average person can distinguish
perhaps 30 or 40 gradations between white and black, although a person
with high acuity (visual sharpness) might be able to see as many as 150
gradations. The colors on the gray scale have no hue and are therefore
termed *achromatic.*

Since most drawings are achromatic, the variations that give mass and
accent are achieved by value alone. The use of value, like the use of color,
can be a personal earmark, and frequently is expressed by the artist's
choice of medium, with ink and charcoal usually the choices for strong
contrasts in value. The individuality possible through use of value can best
be shown in two drawings in the same medium. Let us consider pencil, for
example. The heavy dark lines in the drawing in Figure 157 give it strong
linear quality. Few portions are left white; diverse cross-hatching tech-

158

niques are used to indicate mass and shadow. In the Ingres drawing (Fig. 158) the pencil is used to depict an immensely complex subject with the least possible means. Darks are held to a few crisp accents, and modeling is achieved by sharp lines and a suggestion of shading. The result is one of delicacy, gaiety, and fragile charm.

The gray scale (Pl. 10a, p. 105) is the basis for value in color, for the gradations can be translated into any hue (Pl. 10b, p. 105). The reverse process—a conversion of colors into values of gray—occurs in black-and-white photography (Fig. 159). Values that are not noticeable in a color painting become much more important in a black-and-white photograph of the work.

Every color has what is termed a *normal* value. This has to do with the inherent lightness and brightness of the hue; for instance, yellow is lighter and brighter than purple and will therefore have a lighter normal value. The term *normal* refers generally to the value in the middle of the value scale. This value of a hue is what is represented on a color wheel. Hues at their normal value can themselves be arranged in gradations of value cor-

158
Jean Auguste Dominique Ingres.
Family of Lucien Bonaparte. 1815.
Graphite on white wove paper, 16¼ × 20¼″
(41 × 51 cm). Fogg Art Museum,
Harvard University, Cambridge, Mass.
(Grenville L. Winthrop Bequest).

159
Hudson (Gordon Jackson) and Rose (Jean
Marsh) in a scene from the television
production *Upstairs, Downstairs.*

responding to the gray scale (Pl. 10c, p. 105). Color values that are lighter than normal value are called *tints,* those darker than normal value *shades.* Thus, pink is a tint of red, and maroon is a shade of red. In mixing paints, the addition of white will lighten value and black will darken it.

Intensity, also known as *chroma* or *saturation,* indicates the relative purity of a color. Colors that are not grayed, which are at their ultimate degree of vividness, are said to exhibit *full intensity,* as shown in Plate 11 (p. 105). It is often difficult for students to comprehend intensity. One way of visualizing the meaning is to imagine a jar of powdered pigment in any hue and a saucer of oil into which the pigment will be ground with a mortar and pestle to form paint. When the first portion of pigment is added, the color is weak and diluted, but as the amount of pigment increases, the hue becomes more intense; the oil becomes saturated with pigment and, therefore, with color. The term *low intensity* means that the pigment has been grayed by addition of another color or of black or white. Low-intensity colors are often referred to as *tones,* and they include one of the most useful and subtle ranges of color.

Many dark colors are not only low in value but low in intensity. Maroon, in addition to being a shade of red, is also a low-intensity version of it. Browns are generally low-intensity, low-value yellow-red. Tan is a low-intensity, high-value yellow-red.

A knowledge of how to mix colors is fundamental to the artist. This, again, is both an art and a science and requires a thorough knowledge of the interaction of color.

159

Color Interactions

In all color wheels it is assumed that the two colors directly opposite each other are as different in character as possible. These pairs are called *complementary,* and their special relationship is an important element in creating color harmonies. On the Munsell color wheel, for instance, we note that blue and yellow-red are opposite each other. In Plate 6 (p. 103) we see that Camille Pissarro has used blue extensively for the shadows on grass and trees as well as in depicting the sky. He has balanced the variations of blue with accents of yellow-red in roofs, chimneys, and the capping on the wall. Complementary color harmonies have long been fundamental to the work of painters and interior designers.

In studying color in light rather than in pigment, we find that complements contain the hues known to compose white light. Photographers and printers working in color make use of this fact in formulating the principles of additive and subtractive primaries. The additive primaries are green, red, and blue: this principle is demonstrated in Plate 12a (p. 105). Here white light has been projected simultaneously through gelatin filters, one in each of the three colors. A red filter transmits the color red because the gelatinous film of the filter has absorbed the waves of all other colors. Similarly, a green filter will cast a green light, a blue filter a blue light. When red and green are focused on the same area, the light will be yellow. When green and blue are overlapped, the result is called cyan, or turquoise, and a combination of red and blue is known as magenta. In the area where all three colors overlap, we see white, or *all light,* derived from the three *additive primaries.*

Reversing the process produces *subtractive primaries,* as shown in Plate 12b. Suppose the light were projected through three more filters in magenta, yellow, and cyan. Wherever two areas of light overlapped, we would see an additive primary: green from cyan and yellow, red from magenta and yellow, and blue from magenta and cyan. Where all three overlap there would be not white, but black. When subtractive primaries interact, color is *subtracted* from light.

These principles have a relationship to color in pigment, which we will discuss in more detail later in the chapter. In exploring the interaction of color it is necessary to consider pigment as well as light. For instance, two complements mixed in equal parts in paint do not produce white but a neutral color, usually a variation of gray. However, when the same two complements are placed side by side, they become not grayer, but more intense. This phenomenon is known as *simultaneous contrast.*

The quickest way to understand this term is to take part in one of the experiments of Josef Albers, who made a career of the study of color. If you will turn to Plate 13 (p. 106) you will see two circles, a red one and a white one, each with a small black dot in the center. Fix your eyes on the dot in the center of the red circle and stare at it steadily for perhaps half a minute. Moon-sickle shapes may appear around the periphery, but do not be distracted; continue staring. Now, when your eyes have become thoroughly used to the red circle, quickly switch them to the white one, focusing once more on the little black dot. If you have the usual reaction, you will see a circle that is not white but blue-green, the complement of red.

Albers explained that this reaction is due to the fact that the human eye is tuned to receive any one of the three primary colors of red, yellow, and blue. Staring at red will fatigue the nerve ends in the retina so that a sudden switch to white (which consists of red, yellow, and blue) will register only the mixture of yellow and blue. Thus the eye perceives blue-green, the complement of red. The complement thus seen is called the *after-image*.

Albers' explanation of simultaneous contrast could apply to the increased intensity of adjacent complements. Since we know that mixing colors grays them, we can assume that overlapping them might cause us to see gray. However, when we separate them, looking first at one and then the other, the nerve ends tire of each in turn. Thus, whenever the eye changes, it sees the color it has focused upon without any of the components of its complement. To be specific, if red and blue-green are placed side by side and the eye is concentrated on the red until the nerve ends tire, when the eye is moved to blue-green it will perceive only blue and yellow mixed with no modifying color. The blue-green will therefore be of maximum intensity.

It must be stressed that no one really knows the reasons for the various aspects of color perception. Albers stated unequivocally that color is the most relative medium in art.

Related to simultaneous contrast is another phenomenon known as *successive contrast*. If we were to look at the red circle in Plate 13 (p. 106) and then look at a red circle instead of a white one, we would not see blue-green; instead we would see black. The possible explanation of this is that the fatigued retinal nerve ends see the complement of red (blue-green) but there is no white light to reflect it, so instead they superimpose the blue-green over the red surface, eliminating all light and resulting in black. In successive contrast, then, the afterimage is added to the perceived color instead of reacting to white light. Here again the explanation is purely theoretical.

Still another experiment reinforces the illusory quality of color by demonstrating the *reversed after-image*. This time look at the yellow circles in Plate 14 (p. 106). Once again, fixing your eyes upon the circles, stare fixedly for half a minute or so. Now shift focus suddenly to the white square below the circles. One might logically expect to see purple or blue circles (the complement), but this is not the case. One does not even see circles, but the curved diamond shapes resulting from the difference between the circles and the squares. These are not in the complement but are yellow. Albers characterized this as a double illusion and gave it the name *reversed after-image* or *contrast reversal*.

Objects change color for one of three reasons: a change in the chemical composition of the object, a change in the position of the object in relation to other colored objects, or a change in the source of light. It is this last change that we will now examine.

Lighting and Color

The color of any surface depends to some degree upon its ability to reflect light. The effect of the sun as it progresses across a varied and often moving landscape is one of almost magic complexity. Painters for centuries have tried to capture their impressions of light on land and water and the drama of atmospheric conditions under diverse light. One group of nineteenth-century Americans even called themselves Luminists, making these effects their primary objective (Pl. 15, p. 106).

160

If we responded to every change of color in our surroundings as the result of daylight, we would soon find ourselves exhausted visually and psychologically. We therefore screen out much that happens around us visually, just as we ignore many smells, sounds, and tactile experiences. The artist cultivates these sensations as the materials of creative work and thus acquires a reputation for being unusually sensitive. A painter learns to notice the change in color that occurs when a cloud passes over the sun, or the totally different colors of field and water on a stormy day and on a sunny one, and the variations of green in a blade of grass from its tip to its base.

Artificial lighting has expanded our color experiences into a full-time adventure. At night our world is bathed in yellow or blue light that gives familiar outlines an eerie look. We are no longer startled by spotlighted landmarks rising mysteriously from the darkness with unreal colors accentuating their contours. Most dramatic, of course, is the use of light in the theater. In the circus, a drama, a concert, or an athletic event, light becomes a full-scale medium controlling our attention and pleasure through the use of colored filters, changing spotlights, and alternating beams.

The use of light and chemistry can achieve intriguing *expansion of color,* providing diversity through such illusory qualities as iridescence, luminosity, luster, and transparency. *Iridescence* is the rainbow effect evident in a raindrop or a seashell (Fig. 160), wherein the play of light on the surface color appears to produce all the hues of the spectrum. Iridescence can be difficult to achieve with paint, but many sculptures and constructions, especially in plastic, are iridescent.

160
Turk's cap shell (*Turbo sarmaticus*), from Capetown, South Africa.

161
Deborah Remington. *Capra.* 1974. Oil on canvas, 6'4" × 5'7" (1.92 × 1.7 m). (© Deborah Remington)

Luminosity implies an actual or illusionary glow of light. We can see this effect in a work by Deborah Remington (Fig. 161), in which a subtle modulation of value from white to electric gray brings an aura of mystery to the painting. Remington manipulates oil paint in such a way that light seems to be coming from behind the canvas, casting a glow outward.

Luster in a work of art is the quality of shine or brilliance, the glow of reflected light. Specially formulated luster glazes are common in ceramics, and contemporary metal sculptures often display a high degree of luster (Pl. 16, p. 107). The painter achieves luster effects through the use of glazes of thinned paint built up in successive layers. Touches of gold add to the illusion of luster.

Finally, *transparency* is the appearance of being able to see through a

161

surface to what lies underneath. Albers conducted experiments to achieve this effect through the interaction of colors, but most painters rely on thin layers of paint that reveal masses and shapes underneath. Of course, in other media transparency is implicit in the material, as in Steven Weiss' table in Figure 61 (p. 39).

Color and Pigment

Pigments are substances of various kinds that have been ground into a fine powder to color paints and dyes. Paints are classified not by their pigments but by their *binders*—the substances used to hold them together. Thus, the same pigment that is added to linseed oil to make oil paint can be bound in gum arabic for watercolor, or in acrylic.

Originally pigments came from the earth or from other natural sources. The so-called earth tones got their names during the Renaissance, when they were dug from the soil around the city of Sienna or in the region of Umbria. These pigments retain today the names of raw sienna and raw umber in their natural state or, when baked to give a deeper hue, of burnt sienna and burnt umber. Other colors were taken from plants, sea creatures, or insects. Most pigments today are produced by chemical means; this increases their supply and also improves their durability and intensity.

The designer's approach to color depends upon the medium involved. The absorptive and reflective qualities of pigments can be affected by the binder, so it is necessary to become familiar with a medium by experimentation before definite results can be predicted. Mixing two colors of oil paint, for instance, may yield a result different from that of mixing similar colors in acrylic. Made from chemical components different from those in the traditional media, acrylics frequently have color names such as dioxazine purple or quinacridone red, which are not found in other media. Such innovations require their own rules for mixing.

Whenever pigments are mixed, a certain amount of light is lost. The amount of this loss depends upon both the reflective capacity of the individual pigments and their relationships to one another. The most unified color harmony is *monochromatic,* resulting from variations on a single hue. A computer, dealing with the possible variations of value and intensity, could come up with unlimited combinations within the range of one hue. As we saw in the Albers experiments, pigments most closely related in hue—next to each other on the color wheel—lose the least reflective light and therefore retain most of their brightness or intensity when used next to each other. Since complementary hues are the least chromatically similar of all possible combinations, being opposite each other on the wheel—red and green, for instance—a mixture of two complementaries drastically reduces their intensity so that the result is neutral, usually gray.

In mixing gray itself, awareness of the complements makes possible a whole range of vibrant shades. Black and white may be mixed to produce grays of various values, depending upon the proportions used, but all will be totally neutral. By mixing complements, however, we may produce a neutral that has slight reflective qualities and therefore some intensity—for example, a warm gray resulting from yellow dominating purple or a cool gray from blue and yellow-red, with the blue predominant.

Similar diversity is possible in the range of browns. Any three colors that are equidistant on the color wheel will form a triangle if we draw lines joining them; such colors are known as *triads*. The mixture of three colors in any triad will usually result in brown. This explains why some complements mixed together produce a hue closer to brown than gray, if either has components of the hues next to it on the color wheel. These interactions are inherent in specific media, and the only way to be certain of results is to experiment with the medium to be used.

Psychological Aspects of Color

Psychologists have long known that certain colors have the power to evoke specific emotional responses in the viewer. Among other qualities, colors seem to have a psychological temperature. Red, yellow, and their variations are referred to as warm colors, perhaps because we instinctively associate them with sunlight and fire. Conversely, blue and green—related to forests, water, and sky—are considered cool colors.

Human response to color has become of sufficient importance that people now make careers of color styling, which involves various activities such as designing color schemes for subways or factories and offering counseling services to industrial concerns and small businesses. Color stylists base their services on a thorough knowledge of the relationship of color to human reaction.

In general, warm colors stimulate and cool colors relax. A room with green walls can actually make people feel cold, and office workers have been known to have chills when working in blue surroundings. With the room temperature held constant, the chills lessened when the walls were repainted in yellow or the chairs slipcovered in orange. Employers have also found that their workers produce at higher levels when they are stimulated by bright colors.

The famed Notre Dame football coach Knute Rockne had the locker rooms for his own team painted red and those of the visiting teams painted blue. When halftime came, the visitors instinctively relaxed in their soothing quarters, while the home team remained keyed up and ready for a winning second half. Similar psychology has been adopted in painting the stalls of racehorses, proving that color psychology is not limited to human reaction. Although cats and dogs are color blind, insects react emphatically to color. Mosquitos avoid orange but approach red, black, and blue. Beekeepers wear white to avoid being stung, for they have found that if they wear dark colors, they are besieged. The knowledge that flies dislike blue has helped the meat-packing industry.

Warm colors tend to make objects look closer than cool colors do. For instance, a red chair seems closer than a blue one placed at the same distance from the observer. This knowledge can be useful to the interior designer who needs to alter the apparent size of a room. Painters make use of such knowledge in rendering both landscape and interiors.

Beyond these general, shared responses to color, each individual may react in a special way to particular colors. Each of us brings to the perception of visual stimuli a collection of experiences, associations, and memories that may be triggered by a given color. This could be the color of one's room as a child, or the color of the sky on a special well-remembered day. Color can evoke strong responses, pleasant or unpleasant, and even the viewer does not always understand the reason for the response.

Color Throughout History

The most important fact we need to know about color, whether using it in everyday life or in the profession of designer or painter, is that there are no rules. Even the most scientifically formulated color systems are not infallible, and the full orchestration of color goes much further than any system—its limitless variations and combinations can, like a great symphony, have profound effects upon the human spirit.

Perhaps the best way to comprehend the immense possibilities of color would be to explore its use throughout history. Primitive peoples used earth tones, of course, since the earth was their only source of color. As more sophisticated sources were found, such as marine life and exotic plants, the choices became more arbitrary. Finally, the use of chemistry made selection of color virtually limitless.

In Plates 17 (p. 108) and 18 (p. 109) we see a design and a painting using the same basic hues. Both works are religious in character. Plate 17 is a page from a gospel book done in calligraphy and decorated painstakingly by a monk in a seventh-century monastery on a stony island off the northeast coast of Scotland. It is a part of one of the masterpieces of manuscript *illumination* (decoration), and its beauty lies not only in the tremendous intricacy of the design but also in the subtle use of color to express profound and quiet devotion. Plate 18 is one of the masterpieces of the Spanish painter known as El Greco, who lived and worked in Toledo during the Inquisition in the seventeenth century. Here the forms are writhing human figures, produced by El Greco's unique expression of intense religious fervor. Just as the same musical tones are used in ancient plainsong and in a Bach mass, the same hues have produced these very different visual works created ten centuries apart. However, the Lindesfarne Gospel page employs a red verging on magenta, whereas El Greco uses a deep, luminous red, which radiates from the figure of Christ, the focal point of the painting. The blue of the gospel page is touched with green, like the softness of the sea at evening. El Greco's blue is a regal shade approaching purple. The golds differ as well: the gospel page shines as though touched by sunlight; the painting glows with passion. The closest the two works come to a common interpretation of hue is in the copper color, interspersed throughout the initial letter of the gospel and used, as well, in the figure at the left-hand side of the painting. Throughout the gospel page, the colors are a serene, highly decorative expression. In the painting, El Greco has used them dramatically, their rich tones heightened by dark shadows.

Throughout art history, the use of color has undergone specific changes according to the period and location of designers and artists. In the Renaissance, the painters of Florence, working in a warm, sunny climate, used clear bright colors. At the same time, the painters of Venice on its 120 islands painted with a kind of golden haze typical of the sunlight reflected off the sea and its lagoons. We have discussed the Impressionists' use of color to flood their canvasses with light and give a shimmering surface to their work (Pl. 6, p. 103). One of the most interesting developments in twentieth-century use of color was Color Field painting, which emerged during the late 1940s. With these works we are meant to experience colors directly, since color and form are indistinguishable. There need be no psychological or emotional content in the color, and the artist has deliberately omitted any shape reference that could distract from the purely sensory response (Pl. 19, p. 110). A little later the Op artists emerged as a movement based on the science of optics. Both groups are interested in color not as a means of depicting scenes or objects but as an endless source, in and of itself, of aesthetic possibilities.

Art historians often identify paintings as to period, and even to their painter, by the use of color. In the twentieth century, however, painters are exploring color for its own limitless, and often still inexplicable, qualities. Physicists can tell us about its composition, and psychologists can tell us something about how the eye perceives it. Color stylists tell us how color may affect us physically and emotionally. It is the realm of the artist to reveal perhaps the most important of the many aspects of color, its effect upon the human spirit.

8 Unity and Variety

Having examined the elements of design, we now consider the principles, those guidelines by which the elements are combined into a successful composition. We will consider seven principles governing the organization of any design or work of art. Of these seven, unity and variety are basic and overriding, for no work can function aesthetically without them.

A work devoid of a unifying element is liable to seem haphazard and chaotic. A work that is totally unified, with no variety, can seem boring. These two principles are interlocked. Unity represents the *control* of variety, whereas variety provides the *interest* within unity. In most cases, the ideal objective in a composition is a balance between the two qualities— diverse elements held together by some unifying device. The design in Figure 162 is an excellent example. The thirteen fish and thirteen fowl are all headed in the same direction: this is the first device toward unification. Furthermore, the artist has placed both shapes so the negative shapes resemble the shapes of the opposite species; the spaces between the fowl are similar to the shapes of the fish, and the fish are held together by shapes resembling the fowl. A third unifying device is the diamond shape within which the figures are composed, a variation of the square ground. A fourth is the border of lines that pulls the entire composition together.

Variety also is skillfully handled. Beginning with the shapes at top and bottom, the top goose and the bottom fish are rendered realistically through a detailed depiction of surface texture. Working toward the center,

162

162
M. C. Escher. *Lucht en water I*
(Sky and Water I). 1938. Woodcut,
17⅜ × 17⅜″ (44 × 44 cm).
Haags Gemeentemuseum, The Hague.

163
Great variety can be found in the
types of starfish.

each line of figures becomes more abstract until realism disappears completely and both fish and fowl become intermingling shapes forming an abstract design. The reversal of background—black geese against a white ground and white fish against a black ground—is a means of achieving both unity and variety, since in each case the background flows into the figures in the opposing area. Indeed this example shows us why it is impossible to consider unity and variety separately. Even in as unified a pattern as evenly spaced polka dots, there must be variety, or *contrast* between the color of the dots and their background, for the dots to be clearly visible.

Unity

Examples of underlying unity surround us in the natural world. All people, for instance, look somewhat different from one another, but we have no difficulty in identifying them as people. A collection of starfish (Fig 163) might exhibit different characteristics of color, texture, and even number of points, yet a unity of design—in this case, points radiating from a central body—marks them all as starfish. In creating unity within a composition, the designer may use various techniques, as we have seen. Among the most fundamental is *repetition*.

163

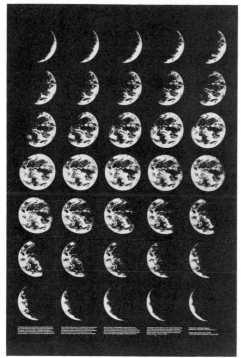

Repetition of motif, shape, pattern, size, or color can create an underlying unity. Repetition of motif, shape, and size are all obvious in the satellite poster in Figure 164. Actually, only the five shapes in the middle row are identical, yet through *closure,* the perceptual completion of a shape, our mind tells us that all the shapes in the poster are the same. The gradual modification of the circular shape, working in from the upper left-hand corner and out again at the lower right, provides not only variety in shape but also a flow of action as the shadow moves across the surface of the planet, yet the variety is secondary to the basic unity of the composition.

A more subtle repetition of shape is used in Renoir's *Le Moulin de la Galette* (Pl. 20, p. 127). Our first impression of this composition is that the canvas seems filled with a colorful *mass* that moves and changes constantly. Upon closer analysis, however, we find that the artist has carefully composed the crowd into a series of triangles. A dancing couple forms a natural triangle, and this motif has been expanded to include the predominant group of large figures in the foreground so that the smaller shapes seem to radiate backward from it. In counterpoint to the triangles are the circular shapes of heads and hats, beginning large in the foreground and shrinking to dots in the background, then repeated with emphasis in the globes of the lighting fixtures overhead. These lights serve an additional function. They repeat the light blue throughout the composition, providing unity through repetition of color.

Unity can be established by harmony of color, texture, or material. The stitchery in Plate 21 (p. 128) exhibits all three. The color is a full range of browns, from beige to orange to deep shades that blend readily into accents of black. The black in turn is lightened into small areas of gray, reaching highlights in white shapes that play throughout the composition. The brown and the black tonal scales thus play in harmony over the surface. Textures are repeated with equal skill, some of them visual, as in the shapes cut from printed fabric and *appliquéd* (stitched onto the background), and some of them tactile, with the interest supplied by tiny stitches. The fabrics are repeated in carefully balanced shapes and intervals, but particular interest lies in the way in which stitches and fabrics echo one another, carrying a theme throughout the composition but with infinite variation.

This type of harmony can be achieved in various media. The great Chinese landscape painters were masters at blending diverse topographical elements (Fig. 165). Their technique was not so much a matter of obvious brushstrokes as of an appreciation of the unity of nature, of Tao, which seeks harmony in all things. In *Buddhist Temple amid Clearing Mountain Peaks,* Li Ch'eng conveys the mysterious unity behind all the elements of the landscape—hills and trees in foreground, the cluster of temple buildings, and the tall, craggy mountains in the background—harmonized by the enveloping softness.

Harmony of *material* can be a unifying device. Sculptor Louise Nevelson concentrated for many years on assemblages of "found" objects—bits of wood, wheels, old newel posts, and other miscellaneous oddments. The fact that they were all of wood contributed unity even to such diverse collections, but the artist used further unifying techniques (Fig. 166). First, she sorted her materials into similar sizes and shapes and then *enclosed* them in boxlike shelves. You will note that some boxes contain thin vertical shapes, others are horizontal in feeling, while others have curved shapes or a combination of shapes. Then she placed each box with great care so the different categories are balanced throughout. Finally, she

164

164
Poster for National Air and Space Museum.
Design: Miho. Earth photos: NASA.
(© 1976 Smithsonian Institution)

165
Attributed to Li Ch'eng (Ying-ch'iu).
Buddhist Temple amid Clearing Mountain Peaks. 10th century. Ink and color on silk, 44 × 22" (1.12 × .56 m). The Nelson-Atkins Museum of Art, Kansas City, Mo. (Nelson Fund).

166
Louise Nelson. *Sky Cathedral.* 1958.
Wood construction painted black,
11'3½" × 10'¼" × 1'6" (3.44 × 3 × .46 m).
Museum of Modern Art, New York (gift of Mr. and Mrs. Ben Mildwoff).

165

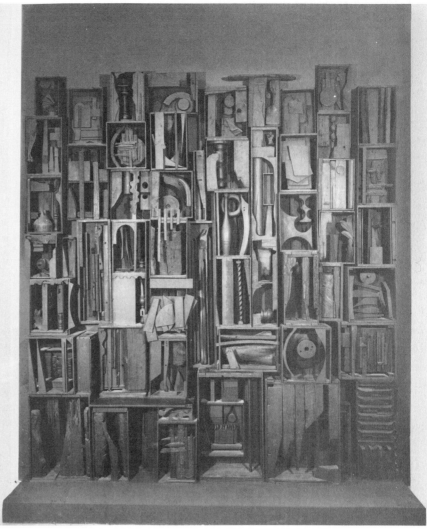

166

painted the entire composition the same color. The result is one of dynamic texture. The Nevelson constructions thus assemble widely varied objects into an intriguing harmony of material, color, and texture.

Variety

The continual change and variety in nature provide the artist with the greatest possible material for design. From the vast storehouse of nature the designer chooses and combines different elements establishing the principle of variety within the context of an original design.

Variations in flowers, rocks, butterflies, animals, and seashells offer such enchantment that people travel the world in search of specimens for their collections. Near at hand, rocks, soil, and dirt roads all have their range of colors and textures derived from mineral deposits, and there is variety in the shape and size of puddles, which glint from changing lights.

167

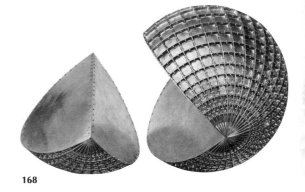

168

Although variety can be very subtle, the essence of variety is *contrast*—rough against smooth, light against dark, large against small. In Figure 167, the photographer used dramatic lighting to emphasize these contrasts. The result is a fascinating interplay of shapes and textures whose relationships seem to shift as we watch. The intense lights and darks flow throughout, unifying the rugged surface into a harmonious composition. This is an excellent example of what we mean by choosing and combining natural elements to establish the principle of variety within unity.

An eloquent expression of both unity and variety through the use of a single material can be seen in the cast aluminum sphere in Figure 168. A simple metal sphere would be unified but would not be interesting; therefore Robert Bart has covered the surface with a fretwork that radiates and expands with the curvature of the mass, the frets being small at the two poles and increasing in size toward the center. What arrests our attention, however, is the slicing open of the sphere, revealing perfectly smooth surfaces within. These now lie exposed and in startling contrast to the patterned exterior, though the use of rivets along the inside edges serves as a transition from the smoothness to the extreme roughness.

167
Minor White. *Capitol Reef, Utah.* 1962.
Photograph. Gelatin-silver print, 12⅛″ × 9¼″
(30.73 × 23.5 cm). Courtesy Minor White
Archive, Princeton University, New Jersey.

168
Robert Bart. *Untitled.* 1965.
Cast aluminum, 12¾ × 17¾ × 17½″
(32 × 45 × 44 cm). Courtesy Leo Castelli
Gallery, New York.

Plate 20
Auguste Renoir.
Le Moulin de la Galette. 1876.
Oil on canvas, 4'3½" × 5'9".
(1.31 × 1.75 m). Louvre, Paris.

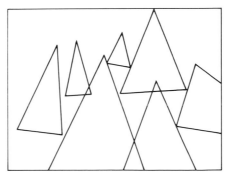

Diagram of Renoir's
Le Moulin de la Gallette.

127   *Unity and Variety*

Plate 21
Martha Mood. *America's First Families.* Post-1967. Stitchery, 36 × 60" (80 × 150 cm).

Plate 22
Cleve Gray. *Threnody.* 1972–73. Acrylic polymer on canvas, filling perimeter of gallery; .
96 × 68 × 22' (29.26 × 20.73 × 6.7 m). Neuberger Museum, State University of New York at Purchase. Courtesy the artist.

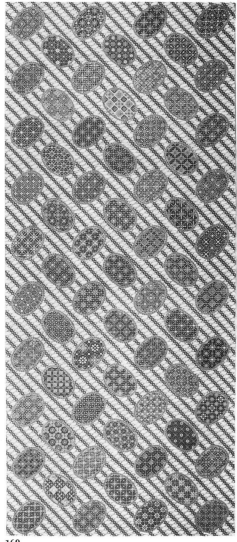

169

In quite another medium, the same principles were an obvious consideration. The textile in Figure 169 was woven and then decorated by the batik method, which has long been a skilled art among the people of Indonesia. This example from Java is done on the diagonal, a form of design considered to be more interesting when worn than designs on the horizontal or vertical axis, and therefore of superior merit. There are two unifying devices here: the allover consistency of the background pattern, and the repetition of identical ovals over the entire surface. As always, the interesting part is the handling of such unified elements to give variety. Every other oval is turned at right angles: this immediately varies the visual pace. Even more important, perhaps, is the fact that each oval is unique, with an individual design unlike that of any of the other ovals on the fabric. This is variety carried to a superlative degree, yet there is nothing chaotic about it, for the regularity of the ovals and their skillful placement guarantee a unified pattern. These careful design considerations have made this particular textile a superb example of the art of batik.

169
Kain panjang. Java, Jogjakarta region. Batik, cotton; warp 8′ (2.45 m), weft 3′4″ (1.04 m). The Sylvia Bishop Collection, Palm Beach, Florida.

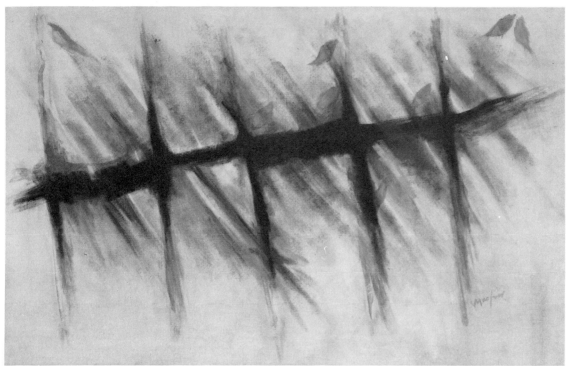

170

In contrast to this complex design is Loren McIver's painting in Figure 170. Here the basic lines are strong and simple, consisting of a slightly slanted line with other lines at right angles to it, which suggest window frames through which light and patterns are revealed. The unity again is obvious, but the variety is achieved by the placement of background lines in an opposing direction. This immediately sets up a tension that is dynamic, implying movement. The addition of a few leaf forms contributes to the reaction of the viewer, tossing out symbols from which to visualize our own concept of how it would seem if we were looking through a skylight. We sense wind, light, and movement—the result of a few strong elements skillfully used.

Variety of form in architecture has appeared in many styles through the centuries, from medieval castles to Victorian homes. The Russian church in Figure 171 displays what may well be the extreme limits of variety in a wooden structure. The series of onion domes reaching upward, the curved niches behind them, and the curved and serrated shingles all represent ways in which wood can be formed and bent with careful skill. Behind this skill, however, lies more than the desire for tremendous variety, for there is an obvious unity in the repetition of the dome shape throughout the structure, and the continuation of the textural richness on both domes and gable. Moreover, the series of crosses on the domes provides not only a symbolic unity but a very real visual thread that unifies the diverse structural masses.

These, then, are some of the ways in which variety and unity can be achieved. With the importance of these two principles in mind, we now move on to other principles we will find closely related and frequently intertwined with those we have just considered.

170
Loren MacIver. *Sky Light.* 1980. Oil on canvas, 26 × 41″ (.66 × 1.04 m). Courtesy Pierre Matisse Gallery, New York.

171
Church of the Transfiguration, Kizhi, USSR. 1714.

131 *Unity and Variety*

9 Balance, Emphasis, and Rhythm

The three principles to be discussed in this chapter are so basic a part of the world around us that they necessarily influence the work of any sensitive designer. Not only are they intrinsic to the environment in which we live, but they are vital to human life itself. As a principle of design, each plays a major role in the achievement of unity.

A particular type of *balance* causes human beings to walk erect, in contrast to most other creatures on the earth. In all forms of life, balance is necessary for survival. For every intake of breath, one must exhale, and periods of activity must be balanced by periods of rest. Science and mathematics are founded on the principle of balance. In an algebraic equation, for example, the two sides must balance. Politicians seek a "balance of power," with political parties balancing one another in order to represent as nearly as possible the will of all the people. We find balance everywhere in the natural world. The cycle of the seasons, the distribution of day and night, and the landscape in which bright sunlight is softened by the blues and greens of field, forest, and water—all display a fundamental balance.

The achievement of a goal, a moment of deep happiness, a visual element that attracts our attention by being spectacular: these provide *emphasis,* being high points that stand out from everything around them. In nature, a violent storm (Fig. 172), a mesa jutting out from the flat landscape, and a mountain peak against the sky are all examples of emphasis. Composers and writers guide their works through a series of emphatic incidents, usually culminating in one great climax from which the rest of the composition takes its significance. Our individual lives are a series of climaxes that stand out in memory because of their influence on the rest of our experience.

Another basic component of the universe we inhabit is *rhythm.* Planets in our solar system have a rhythm of revolution around the sun, as does our moon around the earth. The seasons follow regular rhythms, resulting in a rhythm of sowing and harvesting. Animals, birds, and fish in their migration and breeding habits follow precise rhythms human beings find astounding. Tiny hummingbirds fly from the Canadian border to South Amer-

172

172
Myron Wood. *Plains storm east of Pueblo, Colorado.* 1975. Photograph.

173
Diagrams of three types of balance.

174
Logo for International Harvester. 1973. Design: DeMartin Marona Cranstoun Downes, Inc., New York.

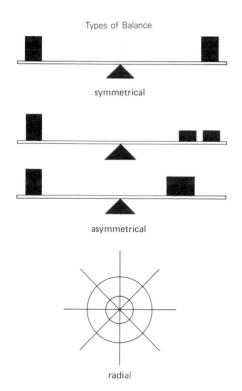

Types of Balance

symmetrical

asymmetrical

radial

173

174

ica each winter, yet arrive back at almost the same moment each year, and each autumn the salmon from deep northern waters fight a heroic struggle through shallow and tumultuous streams to get up to their spawning grounds. When travelers suffer "jet lag" it is because the natural rhythms of the body are upset by flying long distances in a short period of time. Every aspect of our being depends upon such rhythms. The heartbeat and throb of pulse and the regularity of breathing are known as "vital signs" because their rhythms are essential to survival. We can assume that rhythmic movements of the body as expressed in music and the dance are satisfying to us because they respond to a rhythm deep within us.

Since these three principles of balance, emphasis, and rhythm are such a fundamental part of us, it follows that they will be among the most important qualities of any successful design. We will find that they are closely interwoven in the visual arts, for rhythm provides balance, and emphasis is a component of rhythm. We will discuss each one of these principles individually, but we will find that in nearly every case the other two are hovering nearby.

Balance

The absence of balance is usually noticeable and its removal can be catastrophic. If we remove the lowest card in a house of cards or topple the first domino in a line, the structure collapses. Lack of balance in a composition is equally unsettling, making us feel vaguely uneasy. For this reason, artists sometimes deliberately upset our sense of balance in an effort to create a startling effect. For the most part, however, balance is a basic characteristic of a work of art. *Balance of shape and mass* is traditionally divided into three categories: symmetrical, asymmetrical, and radial (Fig. 173).

In *symmetrical* balance, we can draw an imaginary dividing line through the center of a composition so the two resulting halves will form a mirror image of each other (Fig. 174). Another term for this is *bilateral symmetry.* Although we are told that no human body is exactly the same on each side, most human bodies are visually symmetrical, and therefore most things associated with them, such as furniture and clothing, are designed symmetrically. Symmetrical balance comes naturally to most designers. Certainly it is the easiest type of balance to achieve.

A composition that is balanced symmetrically tends to seem stable, dignified, and calm, creating a sense of repose. Most architecture, and especially public architecture, is symmetrical. Colonial and Federal period houses in the United States characteristically had a door set directly in the middle of the façade, with windows evenly arranged on either side and a chimney at each end. It is interesting that young children usually draw their houses in this fashion, as though the inclination toward symmetrical balance were a basic human instinct.

In *asymmetrical* balance, the two imaginary halves of a composition will have equal visual weight, but the forms will be disposed unevenly, as in the second and third drawings in Figure 173. As anyone who has ever played on a seesaw knows, balance can be established by moving backward and forward from the center or fulcrum. It can also be established by distribution of weight. In other words, two small people will balance one large one. Stated mathematically, 2 plus 2 equals 4, but so does 1 plus 3.

175

175
Henri Cartier-Bresson. *Simiane la Rotonde.*
1970. Photograph.

176
John Makepeace, FSIAD FRSA. Storage unit
in birch, acrylic, and stainless steel. 1972.
Pillar of birch plywood and acrylic drawers
cantilevered on a stainless steel column,
height 4'10" (1.48 m). Courtesy the artist.

177
Aequorea, a species of marine life. Carolina
Biological Supply Company.

178
Pier Luigi Nervi and Annibale Vitellozzi.
Cupola and dome, Palazzo dello Sport,
Rome. 1957.

Translated into visual terms, this kind of symmetry can produce a composition like the one in Figure 175. Perhaps the most remarkable thing
about this photograph is not so much the superb balance as the fact that
no one posed for it. No doubt dozens of people walked by without seeing
anything unusual about the scene, but Henri Cartier-Bresson, with his artist's eye, immediately recognized the unique elements and recorded them.
The center of interest, of course, is the two small boys in the foreground,
but they are balanced by the two little girls in their book-end pose *plus* the
textural interest of the peeling wall at the left. Only a trained eye would
have realized the necessity for the expanse of wall. The light patches balance the light panel at the right, pulling the composition together and
complementing the figures of the girls. The arms of the man echo the
triangular shapes of the boys' legs, which are repeated in the letters on the
disintegrating poster.

The storage unit in Figure 176 illustrates both symmetrical and asymmetrical balance. When it is closed, its balance is symmetrical, but the
open position reveals an exciting asymmetry. If symmetry tends to suggest
repose, asymmetry is characteristically active and dynamic. Interior designers use asymmetry to create a more interesting effect in a room, by
balancing two chairs against a sofa, for instance, or a group of small paintings against one large one. This kind of balance involves not just shape and
size but color and texture. An area of rough or interesting texture can
balance a larger area of smooth surfaces.

134 *Design Through Discovery*

Radial balance results when a number of elements point outward from a central core, like the spokes of a wheel. It is found abundantly in nature—in rays emanating from the sun, an age-old symbol of the sun god; in the structure of flowers whose petals follow a radiating pattern; and in the seed structures of such plants as dandelions and milkweed. Many species of zoological life also develop in a radiating pattern (Fig. 177). In architecture, radial symmetry is used widely, in the dome and other circular forms (Fig. 178). It is perhaps the most dynamic type of balance, for it connotes explosive action, like the sparks from a skyrocket that shoot into a breathtaking circular pattern, filling the sky. It further has a connotation of infinity, as do the ripples of water spreading in a pond.

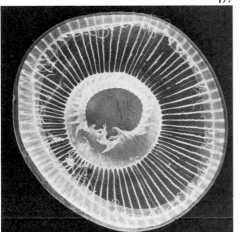

176

177

178

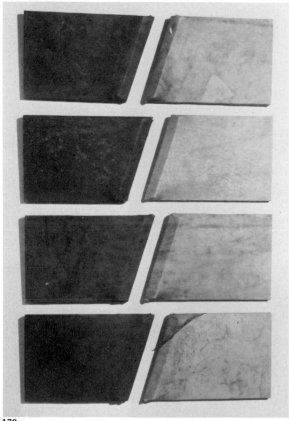

179

180

179
Joe Atteberry. *Zig Zag*. 1980. Rawhide,
tea-stained wall piece,
4'9" × 3' (1.45 × .91 m). Private collection.

180
Robert Rauschenberg. *Summer Rental*. 1960.
Oil and paper on canvas, "combine" painting.
5'10¼" × 4'6" (1.78 × 1.37 m).
Private collection, New York.

181
Residence, on the Gulf of California,
of James T. Flynn, architect AIA.

182
This Japanese garden stresses the
interplay of many natural textures. From
House & Garden Garden Guide;
copyright © 1968 by The
Condé Nast Publications, Inc.

Balance of value simply means a balance between lights and darks in a composition. In the wall piece by Joe Atteberry in Figure 179, the balance is perfectly symmetrical but on a horizontal axis instead of the more usual vertical one. This could be a mechanical division of space and of value except for the texture of the leather, which carries echoes of the light value into the dark areas and marks the light bands with a mottled darkness throughout. Thus the balance is more subtle than is obvious at first glance. In the canvas in Figure 180, the balance is even less clearly defined. Blocks of dark balance blocks of light, but the shapes are quite different and the distribution is not at all symmetrical. An interesting aspect of this composition is the fact that although we usually think of dark as being heavier than light, the darks seem to hang from the top of the canvas, suspended over the large portion of light toward the bottom.

Architects work with values in balance when they design the projections and openings in a building. Any projection from the exterior will create dark values of shadows, which can be balanced against light values where sunlight hits the smooth façade (Fig. 181).

Japanese gardeners have a deep appreciation for *balance of texture.* With twelve centuries of gardening tradition behind them, nearly every family has its garden in Japan, often tiny plots carefully cultivated to express an inborn veneration for nature, which is interpreted in moss, wood, and stones as well as in shrubs and other plantings. The textures of stones and plants are meticulously balanced, as are the varied textures possible through the use of different kinds and sizes of stones (Fig. 182).

181

182

183

Texture is handled in a rhythmic way to provide balance in the work in Figure 183. By laminating thin pieces of wood, the artist has built up a flowing work that almost seems to tie itself in a knot, yet stands firmly in balance on its pedestal. The textures supplied by the varying colors of wood are balanced by four smooth areas and by the dark spots placed in careful balance to one another.

The *balance of color* in design or painting takes its cue directly from nature. Warm, advancing colors—red, yellow, and orange—tend to have more visual weight than the cooler blues, greens, and purples. A painter who is trying to balance a composition in many colors may find that a very small amount of red will be equal to a large field of blue and green. To some extent, we are undoubtedly conditioned to this response because of nature's example. The overwhelming proportion of our landscape is composed of cool colors: the blue of sky and water, the green of grass and trees. Bright, warm colors appear primarily as accents, in birds and flowers. We expect red, for instance, to be either isolated (in a clump of flowers) or transitory (in the flush of sunrise or sunset or the brief glory of fall colors). This may be why we attach more visual weight to bright hues; we notice them more because they are not our customary background.

A composition of predominantly cool colors can, of course, be in perfect balance, as can one of all warm colors. In such cases, the balance is achieved by variety of hue and value, of texture and shape. The relative emphasis of warm and cool is dramatically demonstrated in Barnett Newman's painting in Plate 19 (p. 110), however. Here a field of green is broken by two simple lines, one a clear yellow and the other, wider line a yellow-orange. The lines vibrate against the cool background, drawing our attention not only because of the contrast in color but also because they are the only variations in a field of solid green. The interest they arouse and their strong contrast to the background make for perfect balance.

183
H. C. Westermann. *The Big Change.* 1963.
Laminated pine plywood, 56 × 12 × 12″
(142.2 × 30.5 × 30.5 cm).
Private collection, New York.

184
Jacques Louis David.
The Death of Socrates. 1787. Oil on canvas, 4′3″ × 6′5¼″ (1.3 × 1.96 m).
Metropolitan Museum of Art, New York (Wolfe Fund, 1931).

Emphasis

Certain types of design have no special point of emphasis. These are repetitive and decorative by nature, and we are more interested in the allover effect than in focusing on one part of the composition. Textiles and wallpaper are good examples of this. However, many works of visual art benefit from having a *focal point* or points, some element that attracts the eye and acts as a climax for other sections of the composition, providing the kind of emphasis that is supplied, for example, by the climax in a play. Without such points, our eye is apt to move restlessly through the work, unconsciously searching for something on which to focus. It may be helpful to explore the means by which emphasis is achieved in two very different paintings.

In Jacques Louis David's *Death of Socrates* (Fig. 184), the focal point is obvious: the figure of Socrates himself. Here the artist makes striking use of light and tonality to achieve both emphasis and drama. The body of Socrates is also rigidly vertical, whereas all nine of the men surrounding him lean toward him. The upraised finger is the highest point in the foreground, creating a focal point within a focal point. Furthermore, David has positioned Socrates alone almost at the center of the canvas, whereas all the others are grouped at the sides. Finally, a color reproduction of this painting would show that Socrates alone is dressed in white, whereas his followers are all garbed in cool tones of red, blue, and orange.

184

185

Since David's style was a thoroughly *classical,* intellectual one, his aim was utmost clarity. Francisco Goya could be considered as almost an opposite to David, for his work is characteristically dark, brooding, and strongly emotional, or in other words, *romantic.* Even so, the same emphatic devices operate in his *Executions of the Third of May, 1808* in Figure 185. The figure of the man about to be shot is spotlighted this time, isolated from his fellows by a brilliant glare. He is also dressed in a light color in contrast to the dark garments of the others. His arms are raised in a crucifixion pose, an automatic center of attention. The soldiers' rifles, with fixed bayonets, point directly to him, and the angle of their bodies further directs the viewer's eye in his direction. Perhaps the placement of the figure in the total composition exemplifies as much as anything the difference between the two styles. As a classicist, David has used a formal, almost symmetrical structure for his composition, with the arched doorway and lighted distant figures balancing the weight of the heavier cluster of figures at the right. Goya's composition is spectacularly *asymmetrical,* depending upon the heavy group of figures at the right, interspersed with light accents, to balance the high drama of the central figure to the far left.

In both works five devices were used to achieve dramatic emphasis—light, direction, height, position, and color.

In the design in Figure 186, in contrast, emphasis is achieved primarily through texture. In this terra cotta panel reminiscent of a terraced Greek village, the band of pebbled surface running vertically just left of center becomes the cobbled street. The primary focal point is the textural interest of the pebbles. The appearance of the element of texture in textured clay throughout the composition underscores the textural emphasis of the pebbled band, contributing at the same time a sense of balance.

186

Rhythm

Rhythm is a regular pulsation, like the beating of the heart or a drum beat. Figure 187 shows a visual translation of three rhythmic patterns, the first consisting of regular pulsations, the other two having evenly spaced points of emphasis. One could tap out these patterns with a drumstick or a pencil, giving more intensity to the stronger beats, shown by the larger dots.

Some artists work to the accompaniment of music in order to transmute rhythmic sounds into their work. Others express a natural sense of rhythm without conscious effort, much as rhythm is expressed naturally by a dancer. All expressive processes can set up rhythms, and all works can convey them. In creating a visual design the artist may lend a *physical* rhythm to the application of brushstrokes, the impact of hammer on chisel, the thudding of the shuttle on the loom, or the humming of the potter's wheel. The rhythmic leg motion in working the pedals of a potter's wheel is vitally important to the smooth turning of the pot; in fact, the entire body is engaged in rhythmic motion when a potter or a weaver is at work. On the other hand, in painting or sculpture the rhythms may be purely *visual,* deliberately introduced into the composition to provide the impression of flow and unity.

A textile often combines both kinds of rhythm. The person who wove the twined border in Figure 188 undoubtedly experienced the physical rhythms of weaving. In addition, she has created two varieties of rhythm within her design. The center panel is a geometric version of a *flowing* rhythm, such as we find in waves beating upon the shore or rippling endlessly in a rushing stream. The points provide a continuous series of climaxes balanced by their counterparts as the lines dip downward. The designs at the edges, on the other hand, are beats like the ones in the diagram; only these are chevron shapes, repeated with regularity as though they were marching in carefully paced accompaniment to the flowing rhythm in the center.

Swirling curved rhythms are particularly dynamic, as we associate them with something whirling into a vortex, often beyond human control. We see such rhythms in whirlpools and tornadoes, and experience them in reverse in the music of a symphony or opera when the music builds to a resounding climax. In the filament hanging in Figure 189 we experience these rhythms in a subtler form. In the fine mesh of twisting, turning threads that works downward to the sturdier strands curling at the bottom, there is a sense of continual movement and of culmination.

Like unity and variety, the principles of balance, emphasis, and rhythm cannot be considered separately. In every example in which we have cited one of these principles, at least one of the others is present. The wall piece in Figure 179 with its balance of values is a classic example of a beating rhythm. The Flynn house in Figure 181 shows balance of light and dark but also has a dynamic swirling rhythm, with strong emphasis laid on the light cylindrical shapes. It would be a good exercise to carry this analysis through all the illustrations in the chapter, for in this way it would become clear how closely the principles and elements of design are intertwined. We now come to two more principles that are present in all of the designs we have considered: the principles of proportion and scale.

187
The rhythm of a drumbeat can be interpreted visually as a series of dots. Dots of different sizes indicate variations in rhythm and points of emphasis.

188
Twined border using hooked diamond in rhythmic pattern. Sumba, Indonesia.

189
Kay Sekimachi. Hanging. Multilayer nylon multifilament weave; length 40″ (1.02 m).

188

189

10 Proportion and Scale

Both proportion and scale deal with relative size. *Proportion* usually refers to size relationships within a composition, whereas *scale* indicates size in comparison to some constant, often the size of the human body or the size that we expect something to be. One illustration may help to clarify this difference.

The leather chair in Figure 190 is in *proportion* to the room it occupies. Since the room itself is big, two stories tall, and largely open to the outdoors, the oversize piece appears in fitting proportion to the expansive surroundings. However, as a receptacle for the human body, it expands to a very *large scale.* Seen as a baseball glove, its scale becomes enormous!

Since size is a factor in both proportion and scale, the two often overlap. Something that is too large to be in satisfying proportion to its surroundings could be large in scale as well. Realizing that the two are often inseparable in design, we will nevertheless separate them for individual analysis.

Proportion

It is differences in proportion that make people look different from one another. The proportion of leg length to torso, of waist to height, of shoulder width to length of body—all of these differ widely in human beings. Proportions within our faces give us individuality in appearance also. One person will have a short nose, another big eyes, another high cheek-

190

190
An enormous baseball-glove chair
was selected by interior designer
Ann Hartman for a home in the suburbs of
Washington, D.C. (designed by architectural
firm of Hartman-Cox).

191
René Magritte. *La Folie des Grandeurs.*
1961. Oil on canvas,
39½ × 32″ (100 × 81 cm).
(© Private Collection, USA)

191

bones—all of these are a matter of proportion. Many people would feel quite different if they were two inches taller or shorter, or if they had a different nose or chin. Our proportions become an integral part of our appearance to the world and so, to some degree, determine our personality.

Proportion is usually based on an ideal or a norm. Different cultures have different ideals of what is beautiful, and these ideals are frequently a matter of proportion. Things that are unduly out of proportion jar to some degree, whether we are speaking of a giant, a small painting hung on a vast expanse of wall, a huge pattern in a dress on a diminutive woman, or an overreaction to an imagined verbal insult. This is not to say that disproportion is necessarily bad. Sometimes it is unique and interesting. For this reason, artists frequently and deliberately vary the proportions in a composition to attract attention or create impact (Fig. 191).

Perception of size bears a definite relationship to the distance from which we view it. The size of an object is not the size that projects on the retina of our eye but is supplied by the mind, which works from experience and preconceived judgment. An automobile seen at a distance is smaller than the fire hydrant beside us, yet our subconscious mind establishes the automobile as being big enough to dwarf the hydrant if they were side by side. People visiting New York City for the first time are often surprised that the skyscrapers seem so high, just as we are impressed by the great size of Niagara Falls or a European cathedral when we first see them in person. We are familiar with these sights through pictures, which place them in proportion to a small rectangle we can encompass with a glance. Standing before them, our perception can grasp only a small area at a time; consequently the total picture seems enormous.

192

This distortion of proportion can be a matter of position as well as distance. The pyramids of Egypt were built to overwhelm, to show the greatness of the pharaohs buried within them and to stand as monuments for all time. Even the individual stones are of such scale that human beings climbing upon them look like flies. Their proportion, however, can be a matter of viewpoint. In Figure 192 the great pyramid of Chephren looks so small that the figure in the foreground could reach up and touch the top of it. The reason is that he is standing on the neighboring pyramid of Cheops. Both pyramids are roughly the same height—about 450 feet (137 meters). Because of the unusual angle and the telescoping properties of the camera, the mighty Chephren looks almost like a toy.

The camera does this to us repeatedly on the television or movie screen. Tiny insects loom as giants, and even the cells seen under a microscope are shown in immense size and clarity. Such devices can be instructional and artistically effective. We rely on our perception and its subconscious adjustments to assure us that our world still has its normal proportions.

The Golden Mean

For centuries, the shells of snails have fascinated mathematicians because of their orderly growth pattern. This pattern follows the logarithmic spiral and can be reduced to the same mathematical formula that the ancient Greeks followed in planning their temples, sculpture, and vases. It was included in Euclid's writings and gives explicit form to the Greek belief in the importance of mathematics as a governing force in the universe. This precept was expressed philosophically by Aristotle as the *golden mean*, the virtue that is the median between two vices, as courage is the mean between cowardice and foolhardiness.

Mathematically, the precept is known as the *golden section*. The formula for it would read as follows: $a:b = b:(a + b)$. In referring to the plan

192
Pyramid of Chephren. c. 2570 B.C. Height c. 447′ (136.2 m). Photographed from the pyramid of Cheops.

193
The golden section. $a:b = b:(a + b)$. The proportion of side *a* to side *b* is the same as the proportion of side *b* to side *a* plus side *b*. The smaller rectangle and the larger one are therefore in the same proportion. In the resulting 1:1.618 ratio, 1 represents the square and .618 the rectangle.

194
Ictinus and Callicrates. The Parthenon, Athens. 447–438 B.C.

for a Greek temple, for instance, if *a* is the width of the floor plan and *b* is the length, the proportion of side *a* to side *b* would be the same as the proportion of side *b* to side *a* plus side *b* (Fig. 193). The ratio works out as 1:1.618. It has been noted that such a relationship avoids the obvious mechanical unity of a 1:2 relationship, in which a rectangle would be composed of two squares. The golden section is more subtle, and classical scholars have spent years exploring the many uses to which the ancient Greeks put it—in spaces within temples, as rectangles within which sculpture was composed, as the invisible rectangle encompassing Greek vases.

The outstanding example of beautiful proportion in the history of art is the Parthenon (Fig. 194). In its design flexible units known as modules were used to ensure a unified relationship of each part to the whole building. These modules were not units of measurement as such but variable units, such as the diameter of a column, which would be different for different buildings. Built of blocks of Pentelic marble with no mortar, the Parthenon is a supreme example of Greek subtlety. What appears to be a rectangular building is actually a study in harmonious curves that give the various parts a fluid yet substantial harmony. Sculpture positioned above eye level slopes slightly outward toward the top to compensate for the position of the viewer on the ground. The columns are thicker and closer together at the corners because they are seen against the sky and would otherwise appear to be slimmer than the rest. Individual columns curve outward slightly toward the center because if they were straight the weight of the upper part of the building would make them appear to buckle. Numerous other refinements contribute to the graceful proportions that are still evident even in the temple's present deteriorated state.

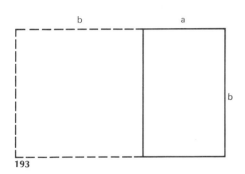

193

194

195

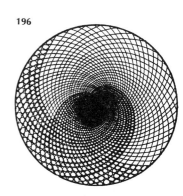

196

The Fibonacci Series

We have continually stressed the design inspiration to be found in nature, but none is more exciting than the discoveries related to the snail shell and the logarithmic spiral upon which the golden mean is based. This ratio was the subject of intensive study during the Renaissance and was no doubt an influence on Leonardo da Pisa (Leonardo Fibonacci), medieval Europe's greatest mathematician, who in the early thirteenth century developed the so-called Fibonacci series. This is a progression of numbers that has been found to reveal the secret of much of nature's structural design, particularly in the field of botany. The progression runs as follows: 1, 1, 2, 3, 5, 8, 13, 21, 34, 55, 89, 144, and so on, with each number being the sum of the two numbers preceding it. It has been found that pine cones have 5 and 8 rows of seeds, pineapples have 8 and 13, dandelions 13 and 21, daisies 21 and 34, and sunflowers 55 and 89 (Fig. 195). Count the leaves on a stem, starting at the bottom; when you reach one that is directly over the one you started with, it will be one of Fibonacci's numbers.

To understand what is meant by the logarithmic spiral, one must draw a

195
Paul Caponigro. *Sunflower.* 1965.
Photograph. Private collection.

196
Seed structure of a sunflower.

197
The logarithmic spiral is based on arcs of circles, which in turn, are based on squares of graduating size.

198
Radiograph of a nautilus shell.

rectangle that has the relationship of 0.618 on one side to 1 on the other. By drawing a diagonal line from one corner, you will arrive at a perfect square. This is not unusual, but there is a unique feature: the remaining rectangle will be in exactly the same proportions as the original one. If one continues this process with increasingly smaller rectangles, the space eventually becomes too small to draw in. Now, if a curve is swung through each square from the inside out, the result (Fig. 197) will be exactly the shape of the chambered nautilus (Fig. 198). Nautilus and snail shells increase on the outward edge so that they grow in size but do not change shape. Many other natural forms grow in size but do not change proportion—the tusks of an elephant, the horns of a ram, and the claws of a cat, for instance. All of these reflect the logarithmic spiral in their final form. It is easy to see how one might become fascinated by such research, finding that so much in nature is based on a single law of proportion.

Few contemporary designers work consciously with a formula such as the golden section, yet many painters have done studies based on the square. Josef Albers' painting in Figure 87 is based entirely on the pleasing proportional relationships between squares of various sizes and their rela-

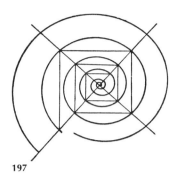

197

198

tionship to the canvas. Other painters have used the square and circle together in a variety of proportional relationships. In Jasper Johns' *Target with Four Faces* (Fig. 199) one circular motif dominates the field, but with bands of color repeated within it, so that the whole establishes a satisfying relationship with the square.

In Plate 22 (p. 128) Cleve Gray does not create paintings to hang on a wall. The paintings *are* the wall. Gray states that he has sought to return to "that early moment when man's experience of totality preceded his experience of the particular." To accomplish this, he has filled the four walls of the room with a continuous color, joining fourteen figures in a dance of death and life around the room. Gray sees the room as an environment for meditation where one can enter and possess one's own thoughts, as in a cathedral. In such a context, there can be no question of the appropriateness of the proportions.

The matter of proportions within a composition is a kind of *hierarchy,*

199

199
Jasper Johns. *Target with Four Faces.* 1955. Encaustic on newspaper over canvas, 26″ (66 cm) square, surmounted by four tinted plaster faces in wood box with hinged front, overall dimensions, 33⅝ × 26 × 3″ (85 × 66 × 8 cm). Museum of Modern Art, New York (gift of Mr. and Mrs. Robert C. Scull).

200
Last Judgment. 12th century. Mosaic, west wall, Cathedral at Torcella, Venice.

200

like the star system in the theater. One element frequently is the most important and all others are subordinate to it, in varying degrees of importance. In the Johns painting (Fig. 199) the targetlike circle dominates, with the faces as supporting actors, so to speak. The title calls our attention to them and we are pleasantly surprised because we didn't really notice them at first.

An even more obvious use of hierarchical proportion characterizes the mosaic in Figure 200. Here proportion is a function of *symbolism*. The figures of Christ and two angels are disproportionately large, their exaggerated size being an indication of their importance. Their size also balances the composition, since the angels are placed at either corner, echoing the dominant figure of Christ in the center.

151   *Proportion and Scale*

Scale

In discussing large or small *shapes* on a two-dimensional surface, we have spoken of proportion, since the shapes are in *proportion* to the size of the area—paper, canvas, or wall—on which they appear. *Masses* are seen in *scale* with their surroundings or with human beings viewing them, for this is a matter of *comparison* rather than of relationships inherent in the work.

The heads shown in Figure 201 are among thousands found on Easter Island in the South Pacific, all similar in size and style. First discovered in 1722, these statues were described in detail by Captain James Cook when he visited the island in 1774. Centuries of drifting silt have buried many of them up to their necks, but they are actually full figures—some over 30 feet (9.1 meters) high. Who carved the megaliths and when and why are questions that remain unanswered. Perhaps the most baffling question is how a tribe with only primitive stone tools managed to erect such heavy structures. One romantic theory suggests a tribe of giants who planned the images in their own likeness—in other words, what to them was natural scale. A more likely explanation assumes that these are ancestor images, elevated to superhuman scale by death. At the time of Captain Cook's voyage, most of the figures were standing upright, but later the inhabitants of the island toppled all those that were not buried. Again, the reasons for this are not clear. In any event, it is the mammoth scale that makes these Easter Island carvings remarkable.

Contemporary uses of scale can have the same goal—to make a work remarkable. The composition in Figure 202 was created for an advertising

201
Stone images. 17th century or earlier. Height 30′ (9.14 m). Located outside crater of Rano Raraku, Easter Island.

202
Photo created by Brand Advertising as a part of a campaign for Safety-Kleen, a company that specializes in recycling waste industrial products. © 1981, Denise R. Tegtman.

campaign by a company that specializes in recycling industrial solvents. Although the Statue of Liberty is depicted by a live model standing in a 55-gallon drum in the middle of a plastic-lined pool, the photographers manipulated the scene to produce the compelling picture of the statue gradually sinking beneath a New York harbor filling up with sludge. Even though the actual monumental statue is impressive, this picture showing the upper part of her body at huge scale sends out a message that is difficult to ignore.

Clean up your act, America.

203

204

203
Stephen Lowe. *The Hermit.* 1972.
Chinese watercolor on rice paper,
37 × 23″ (94 × 58 cm).
Private collection.

204
Rockwell Kent. *Voyaging.* 1924.
Chiaroscuro wood engraving on maple in
black, white, and olive green; 6″ (15 cm)
square. National Gallery of Art,
Washington, D.C. (Rosenwald Collection).

205
John Tenniel.
Alice after Taking the Magic Potion,
illustration from *Alice's Adventures in
Wonderland* by Lewis Carroll,
written in 1865.

206
Big Bird, Susan (Loretta Long), and Bob
(Bob McGrath) in front of the brownstone
set for ''Sesame Street.'' Courtesy
Children's Television Workshop.

Just as the Venetian mosaic in Figure 200 expresses Christian faith by depicting Christ in larger proportions than the other figures, the Chinese characteristically express a veneration for nature by showing the human figure as a minute entity amid the awesome beauty of a natural setting. In the painting in Figure 203, the single figure moves through the landscape like a tiny speck, compared to which even the bark of the pine tree looks enormous. A contrast can be made with a Western treatment of the human wanderer in Rockwell Kent's *Voyaging* (Fig. 204). Here it is the man who is important, the conqueror of mountains. Nature awaits his conquest.

Many people are fascinated by miniature scale. At one time, there was a craze for engraving documents on the head of a pin—the Lord's Prayer or the Gettysburg Address, for instance. To read the words, one needed a strong magnifying glass. A less drastic devotion to the miniature is shared by people who collect dollhouses and their furnishings or who make a hobby of model railroads. Few people can resist the charm of an object that is perfect in every way yet tiny in scale.

Four generations of children have been intrigued by Lewis Carroll's story of *Alice's Adventures in Wonderland,* which centers around her changing scale from very small to very large (Fig. 205). The possibilities that arise from changing scale in relation to one's environment are tantalizing. Carroll explores the advantages and disadvantages with whimsical humor.

Another contemporary figure whose role depends on scale is Big Bird, the genial character around whom much of the action in "Sesame Street" revolves (Fig. 206). The fact that he is out of scale with the rest of his species gives him the special quality needed for his unique function.

205

206

207

207
Scene from Act I of Richard Wagner's
Parsifal. Produced by Wieland Wagner.
Bayreuth Festival, Germany. 1968.
Collection: Bildarchiv Bayreuther
Festspiele.

208
Thomas Cole. *The Course of Empire:
Destruction.* 1836. Oil on canvas,
39¼ × 63½″ (99.7 × 161.3 cm).
The New-York Historical Society,
New York.

The use of scale in theater is legendary, since drama can be heightened
by the use of immense scale in a setting, which can dwarf the actors as
Chinese paintings do. In Wieland Wagner's production of *Parsifal,* this use
of scale is particularly striking. The manipulation of both lighting and scale
convey the solemnity and sense of the supernatural in the quest for the
Holy Grail (Fig. 207).

Just as lighting enhances the scale in the Wagnerian production, lighting
and tonality can be allied to scale in painting. Look again at the Stephen
Lowe painting in Figure 203. The entire composition is wrapped in white,
which seems to drift through the trees and surround the figure. We feel that
the hermit is moving through a mysterious world filled with mist, totally
alone in a vast universe. This sense of the supernatural is partly a matter of
scale, as we stated, but it is also in large part the result of the artist's skilled
use of tonality. It is the sharp darks of the trees standing out from the misty
whites that make us feel the infinite spaces and the aloneness of the figure.

In the painting by Thomas Cole in Figure 208, both large and small
scale are used effectively. The subject itself is immense: the Roman Empire
being destroyed by fire and battle. In order to depict such a catastrophe, it
was necessary to use comprehensive symbols of an entire nation, next to

which any individual element in the painting would be proportionately small. The exception is the statue in the right foreground, which is used to throw the rest of the composition into scale. There can be no doubt that the effectiveness of the work relies heavily upon tonality, the manner in which the artist has dramatized the inferno, highlighting certain spots, plunging others into darkness. The tonality of the statue is particularly eloquent. The back toward the viewer is struck with light, but the side facing the destruction is partially obscured by darkness.

As we have seen, the elements and principles of visual design interweave and flow together, becoming interdependent components of the total composition. Not all of them will necessarily appear in any one composition, but they form a body from which the designer can choose; they are the tools with which one works to create a successful design.

208

Glossary

Terms italicized within the definitions are themselves defined in the Glossary.

abstraction Originating with a recognizable form but simplified or distorted into a new entity.

achromatic Having no color, a *neutral* such as black, white, or gray.

acrylic A *plastic* that in solid form is usually rigid, clear, and transparent; also, a binder for pigments used in painting.

additive Descriptive of a sculptural method in which *form* is created by building up materials, as by modeling or welding. Compare *subtractive*.

additive primary colors In light, those primary colors—red, blue, and green—which in theory can be blended to add up to white light.

aesthetic From Greek *aisthetikos*, "pertaining to sensory perception."

after-image A physiological phenomenon in which the retina of the eye becomes fatigued after viewing any *hue* for a sustained period of time, causing the *complementary color* to be seen.

analogous Referring to adjacent colors on a color wheel.

appliqué A fabric-decorating technique in which various shapes, colors, and types of material are stitched onto a background to create a design.

arch A structural device, generally any opening spanned by a curved top supported by two uprights. The true arch consists of wedge-shaped blocks converging on a keystone at the center of the opening.

Art Nouveau A decorative style of the 1890s, based primarily on flowing, curvilinear plant and animal forms.

assemblage The act of creating a work of art by joining together fragments of objects that often serve some other purpose; also the work so created.

asymmetrical balance Balance in which the two imaginary halves of a composition have equal weight but are disposed unevenly.

atmospheric perspective The effect of an intervening body of air between an object and a viewer, causing a softening of outlines, blurring and cooling of colors, and loss of detail at the horizon; the simulation of depth in two-dimensional art by the portrayal of this effect.

bas-relief or **low-relief** Sculpture in which the figures are attached to a background and project only slightly from it.

batik A form of resist dyeing for fabric in which nonprinting portions of a design are "stopped out" with wax to prevent color penetration.

Bauhaus A school of design founded in Germany, in 1919, known for its adaptation of design principles to mass production; also descriptive of the works, especially furniture, designed by the staff.

bilateral symmetry A type of design balance in which the two halves of a composition, formed by a bisector, are mirror images of each other.

binder A substance in paints that causes the pigment particles to hold together, to a *support*.

biomorphic Taken from nature, from the Greek meaning "structure based on life."

calligraphy The art of beautiful writing.

cantilever A structural member, as in architecture, projecting from an upright, and unsupported at the opposite end.

cartoon A drawing made to scale on paper, used in transferring designs as a basis for painting, mosaic, or tapestry.

casein A painting medium in which the pigment is bound with milk curd.

casting The process of forming a liquid or plastic substance into a specific shape by pouring it into a mold and allowing it to harden.

chiaroscuro The use of light and dark value areas in a painting to imitate effects of light and shadow found in nature.

china A commercial white ceramic ware similar to *porcelain*, firing in higher temperature ranges.

chroma See *intensity*.

closure The process by which perceptions are unified to acknowledge a specific shape.

collage A predominantly two-dimensional work of art on which pieces of paper, cloth, or other materials are pasted. Loosely, any assembly of materials to create a design.

Color Field painting Works in which the viewer is meant to experience colors directly, without reference to form or emotional and psychological content.

color wheel A circular arrangement of colors that expresses their relationships according to a particular color theory.

complement See *complementary colors*.

complementary colors Colors opposite one another on a *color wheel*, which, when mixed together in equal parts, form a neutral, or, in the case of light, form white.

composition An ordered relationship among parts or elements of design.

conceptual art A work of art or an event that depends on an intellectual concept of the artist.

conceptual imagery Imagery derived from imagination, emotion, dreams, or other internal sources; compare *perceptual imagery*.

content The substance of a work of art, including its emotional, intellectual, symbolic, thematic, and narrative connotations.

contour In two-dimensional art, a line that represents the edge of a form or group of forms.

cross-hatching A series of intersecting sets of parallel lines used to indicate shading or volume in a drawing.

Cubism An art style developed by Pablo Picasso and Georges Braque, beginning in 1907, characterized by faceted forms, flattened *pictorial space*, and *figure-ground ambiguity*.

decorative design Embellishment or surface enrichment of an object. Decorative design may be inherent in structure or may be applied to a completed structure.

earthenware A coarse, porous, usually reddish ceramic ware fired in low temperature ranges.

eclecticism The combining of many different styles and influences in one work.

embroidery The technique of decorating fabric with colored threads worked in a variety of stitches.

enameling The art of creating designs in colored glassy materials which are fused to metal.

encaustic A type of paint in which the *binder* is wax.

engraving A technique in which an image is created by scratching into metal, wood, or other materials, with a sharp tool. Also, the *print* that results when ink is placed in the depressions and paper forced in to make an impression.

etching A *printmaking* process in which acid acts as the cutting agent. A metal plate is coated with acid resist; the resist is scratched away in image (or printing) areas, and then the plate is dipped in acid.

Expressionism An early twentieth-century art movement that emphasized the artist's emotional response to experience, especially through the use of color and symbolic imagery.

façade The exterior, usually the front, of a building.

Fauvism A movement in painting, originating in France in 1905, characterized by the unconventional, apparently arbitrary use of bright, contrasting colors.

fiber A natural or synthetic material capable of being made into yarn or thread.

figure-ground A relationship, usually in two-dimensional art, between a form and its background or surroundings. Figure-ground ambiguity refers to an inability to distinguish between the two.

foreshortening A device used in two-dimensional art to portray forms in such a way that they appear to project or recede from the picture plane; a means of creating spatial depth in figures.

form 1. The underlying structure or *composition* in a work of art. 2. The shape or outline of something. 3. The essence of a work of art—its medium or mode of expression. 4. The substance of something, as in "solid or liquid form."

fresco A painting *medium* often used for murals in which the paint is applied to a *ground* of wet plaster.

gesso A mixture of white pigment, glue, and plaster or gypsum that serves as a *ground* for tempera.

Gestalt A term referring to the totality of unified configurations with which we seize our visual experiences, from the German word for "form."

glaze A glassy vitreous coating fired onto ceramic ware for decoration and/or waterproofing. Also, a thin layer of paint, applied to canvas or other base in one or more layers, to achieve transparency or luminosity in a painting.

gouache Opaque watercolor paint in which the *binder* is gum arabic and a paste of zinc oxide.

graphic Descriptive of the arts involving drawing or writing. "Graphic design" usually means design for a printed format, such as advertising, books, magazines, and packaging.

gray scale A series of *value* gradations between white and black.

ground 1. A preliminary material applied to a *support* as preparation for the drawing or painting *medium*. 2. The background or general area of a *picture plane* as distinguished from the forms or figures. See *figure-ground*.

grout Thin mortar or paste used to fill in around the *tesserae* in a mosaic.

hatching A series of closely spaced parallel lines used to indicate shading or volume in a drawing.

haut-relief or **high-relief** Sculpture in which forms project from a background to considerable depth.

hue The pure state of any color; the name by which a color is called.

iconography 1. The visual imagery used to convey the meaning of a work of art, and the conventions governing such imagery. 2. The study of various forms of meaning found in pictorial representations. 3. Loosely, the "story" behind a work of art, especially religious or mythological symbolism.

ideographic A term for writing in which the characters are abstracted images of the objects they represent.

illumination The art of decorating manuscripts with scrolls, miniature paintings, and symbolic embellishments.

imagery The art of making images or pictures to represent or evoke a particular thing. See also *perceptual imagery, conceptual imagery.*

impasto The thick application of paint to a *support;* also, the three-dimensional surface that results from such application.

Impressionism An art style, originating in France in the 1870s, in which artists sought to represent, in paint, transitory effects of light, shade, and color that occur in nature.

intensity The relative purity or grayness of a color. Colors that are not grayed have "high intensity" whereas grayed colors have "low intensity."

interior decoration The arranging of interior furnishings to satisfy a specific taste.

iridescence The rainbow effect by which a material or surface seems to reflect all the hues of the spectrum, as a result of light playing on it.

kinetic Relating to or produced by motion.

lamination Gluing together of thin sheets, as in wood or plastic.

leather hard The stage at which drying clay can be carved or incised.

linear perspective A system for depicting three-dimensional depth on a two-dimensional surface, dependent on the illusion that parallel lines receding into space converge at a point, known as the *"vanishing point."*

lithography A *planographic* or flat-surface *printmaking* technique, in which the image areas are neither depressed nor raised. (Compare *relief.*) Printing depends upon the mutual antipathy of grease and water.

local color The color of things seen under standard light without shadows; the "real" color of objects in the natural world.

logo An insignia adopted by a commercial concern for visual identification in the eyes of the public.

low-relief See *bas-relief.*

luminal art Art, especially sculpture, of which light is an element.

Luminists A group of painters who interpreted the effects of light on colored objects.

luminosity The actual or illusory effect of giving off light.

luster The glow of reflected light.

medium 1. The material used for a work of art. 2. The basis for a type of paint, such as oil. 3. The form of expression in a work of art, such as painting or printmaking.

Minimal Art A style of painting and sculpture, originated

in the mid-twentieth century, in which *form* is achieved by the barest means—contour shape, flat surface, and sometimes pure unmodulated color. Minimal works tend to be geometric in their precision.

modeling 1. Shaping objects from *plastic* material, such as clay. 2. In drawing or painting, effects of light and shadow that create the illusion of three-dimensional volume.

modular Characterized by repetitive and/or interconnecting units that can be assembled in different ways, especially in furniture or architecture.

monochromatic Having only one hue, possibly with gradations of value or intensity.

monoprint A one-of-a-kind *print* made by transferring to paper an image drawn on a plate, usually of glass.

mosaic An art form in which pieces of glass, ceramic tile, or other materials are fitted together to form a design and then glued or cemented to a background.

motif An element, frequently the theme, of a work of art, which may be repeated or elaborated on.

negative space The space surrounding or flowing through the shapes and masses delineated by the artist. See *positive space.*

neutral A color not associated with any particular *hue,* for instance gray or tan.

nonobjective Having no resemblance to natural forms or objects.

nonrepresentational See *nonobjective.*

normal value The value of any color when it is in its pure unmixed state.

Op Art An art style of the mid-twentieth century, concerned with optical stimulation and manipulation, including the creation of optical illusions, a sense of vibration, and *after-images.*

palette 1. The range of colors used for a painting. 2. The range of colors characteristic of a single artist or group of artists. 3. The surface on which an artist mixes paint.

perceptual imagery Imagery derived from experience or perception of the natural world.

pictorial space In a painting, the apparent or illusionary space that appears to recede backward from the *picture plane.*

picture plane An imaginary flat surface assumed to be at the front surface of a painting.

pigment A colorant ground into a fine powder and used to color paints or dyes.

pile weave A weave characterized by protruding tufts or loops of fiber.

pinching A method of shaping clay with the fingers.

plain weave A basic weave characterized by a regular alternating sequence of one-up, one-down interlacing of *warp* and *weft* yarns.

planography A *printmaking* method in which the printing surface is flat, neither raised nor recessed. See *lithography*.

plastic 1. Capable of being molded or shaped. 2. Solid, sculptural, three-dimensional. 3. Any of numerous synthetic substances composed principally of carbon compounds in long molecular chains.

plasticity The ability of a material to be molded or shaped; solidity, three-dimensionality.

plywood Laminated wood in which the grain of alternate layers is at right angles to that of the layers between.

pointillism A technique of applying tiny dots of color to canvas. The term is used especially in connection with the work of Georges Seurat.

polychrome Painting in many colors, as in wood or ceramic sculpture.

Pop Art An art style dating from the mid-1950s that takes as its subject matter popular, mass-produced symbols.

porcelain A pure white, hard ceramic ware that fires at very high temperatures, used especially for fine dinnerware and figurines.

positive space Space occupied by the shapes or masses delineated by the artist. See *negative space*.

post-and-lintel A structural system in architecture in which beams or lintels are placed horizontally across upright posts.

Post-Impressionism A loose term to designate the various painting styles following *Impressionism,* during the period from 1885 to 1900. The term is applied primarily to the works of Van Gogh, Cézanne, Gauguin, Seurat, and their followers.

primary color One of the basic colors on any *color wheel,* which it is assumed cannot be mixed from other colors, and which serves as a basis for mixing all combinations on the wheel.

print An impression made on paper from a master plate, stone, or block created by an artist, usually repeated many times for multiple images that are identical or similar. Also, a similar process applied to cloth.

printmaking The art of making prints.

proportion Size or weight relationships among structures or among elements in a single structure. Compare *scale*.

quilting The process of sewing together small pieces of cloth (in a pattern or at random) to form a design, and then stitching to create a puffed surface.

radial symmetry Balance achieved by the arrangement of elements in a circular pattern around a central core.

refraction The bending of a ray of light as it passes through a prism or lens.

relief 1. A *printmaking* process in which portions of the image to be printed are raised above the surface of the plate or block. 2. Any raised image, as in sculpture.

relief sculpture Sculpture attached to a background from which it projects. See *bas-relief, haut-relief*.

repoussé A forming technique for metal in which punches driven by hammers push the metal out from its reverse side to create a *low-relief* design on the front.

Romantic architecture Architecture with a flavor of fantasy, often Gothic in derivation.

saturation See *intensity*.

scale Size or weight relationships in a structure or between structures, especially as measured by some standard, such as the human body.

secco A method of painting in which plaster is applied to dry plaster walls.

secondary color A color created by mixing two primary colors on any *color wheel*.

serigraphy A printmaking process based on stencils or screens. See *silk screen*.

shade A variation of any color that is darker than its *normal value*.

silk screen A *printmaking* method in which the image is transferred to paper or cloth by forcing ink through fine mesh screens, usually of silk, on which nonprinting areas are "stopped out" to prevent color penetration.

simultaneous contrast The tendency of *complementary colors* to intensify each other when placed side by side.

slab construction A method of forming clay by rolling it into flat sheets and then joining the sheets to each other or to other forms.

slip Liquid clay, the consistency of cream, usually used for casting.

split complement A combination of colors involving one *hue* and the hues on either side of its *complement* on a *color wheel*.

stained glass Glass that has been colored and arranged in pieces to create a design or pattern. Often the pieces are joined by strips of lead.

stitchery Any fabric-decorating technique in which the thread stitches predominate on the surface and carry the major design.

stoneware A relatively hard, vitreous ceramic ware, usually gray or tan, that fires in the middle-range temperatures.

structural design Design concerned with the creation of basic *form* in an object, as distinguished from surface enrichment.

stylization The simplification of a form to emphasize its design qualities.

subtractive Descriptive of a sculptural method in which *form* is created by carving or cutting away material. Compare *additive*.

subtractive primary colors The colors—cyan (turquoise), magenta, and yellow—which subtract from white light the wavelengths for all colors except the one seen.

successive contrast The phenomenon by which the *after-*

image of a visual impression appears to the closed eye, in the complementary colors of its original.

support In two-dimensional art, the material to which the drawing or painting *medium* is applied, as a canvas.

Surrealism An art movement, originating in the early twentieth century, which emphasized intuitive and nonrational ways of working as a means of recreating the chance relationships and symbols that often occur in dreams.

tapestry A type of *weaving* in which the *weft* yarn carries the design and appears on the surface of the fabric only in certain areas.

tempera A painting *medium* in which the pigment is bound together with egg yolk or with animal or vegetable glue.

tensile strength A characteristic of metal, or other materials, whereby it can be stretched or extended without breaking.

terrazzo Small marble chips set in concrete and polished.

tesserae Small pieces of glass, tile, stone, or other material used in a *mosaic*.

thermoplastic Descriptive of *plastics* that can be reheated and reshaped without undergoing chemical change.

thermosetting Descriptive of plastics that undergo a chemical change during curing and become permanently shaped.

tint A variation of any color that is lighter than its *normal value*.

tonality The quality of lightness or darkness, brightness or grayness in a work.

tone A softened color achieved by mixing a pure *hue* with gray or with its *complement*.

triad Any group of three colors equidistant from each other on a *color wheel*.

value The lightness or darkness of a color.

vanishing point In *linear perspective*, the point at which lines or edges parallel in nature converge at the horizon line.

vault An *arched* roof, usually of stone or concrete, created by two intersecting arches.

vehicle See *binder*.

veneer A thin layer of fine wood applied over a base of stronger, less decorative wood. Also applies to marble and other materials.

visual texture Surface variety that can be seen but not felt with the fingers.

warp In *weaving*, the lengthwise yarns held stationary on the loom and parallel to the finished edge of the fabric.

watercolor A painting *medium* in which the *binder* is gum arabic.

weaving The process of interlacing two sets of parallel threads, held at right angles to each other, to form a fabric.

weft In *weaving*, the crosswise yarns that intersect the *warp* to create a fabric.

woodcut See *relief*.

Bibliography

Elements and Principles of Design

Albers, Anni. *On Designing*. Middletown, Conn.: Wesleyan University Press, 1971.

Albers, Josef. *Interaction of Color*. New Haven: Yale University Press, 1975.

Arnheim, Rudolf. *Visual Thinking*. Berkeley: University of California Press, 1969.

Birren, Faber. *Light, Color, Environment*. New York: Van Nostrand Reinhold, 1969.

Collier, Graham. *Form, Space, and Vision*. 3rd ed. Englewood Cliffs, N.J.: Prentice-Hall, 1972.

Evans, Helen Marie. *Man the Designer*. New York: Macmillan, 1973.

Faulkner, Ray, and Edwin Zeigfeld. *Art Today*. 5th ed. New York: Holt, Rinehart and Winston, 1969.

Grillo, Paul. *Form, Function, and Design*. New York: Dover, 1975.

Itten, Johannes. *Design and Form*. 2nd rev. ed. New York: Van Nostrand Reinhold, 1975.

———— *The Art of Color*. New York: Van Nostrand Reinhold, 1974.

———— *The Elements of Color*. New York: Van Nostrand Reinhold, 1970.

Kepes, Gyorgy. *Language of Vision*. Chicago: Paul Theobald, 1969.

Knobler, Nathan. *The Visual Dialogue*. 3rd ed. New York: Holt, Rinehart and Winston, 1980.

Libby, William Charles. *Color and the Structural Sense*. Englewood Cliffs, N.J.: Prentice-Hall, 1974.

McHarg, Ian. *Design with Nature*. Garden City, N.Y.: Natural History Press, 1969.

Nelson, George. *Problems of Design*. 3rd ed. Whitney Library of Design, 1974.

Ocvirk, Otto G., Robert O. Bone, Robert E. Stinson, and Philip R. Wigg. *Art Fundamentals: Theory and Practice*. 4th ed. Dubuque, Iowa: Wm. C. Brown, 1981.

Pearce, Peter. *Structure in Nature Is a Strategy for Design*. Cambridge, Mass.: MIT Press, 1978.

Russell, Stella Pandell. *Art in the World*. New York: Holt, Rinehart and Winston, 1975.

Stix, Hugh, et al. *The Shell: Five Hundred Years of Inspired Design*. New York: Ballantine, 1972.

Strache, Wolf. *Forms and Patterns in Nature*. New York: Pantheon, 1973.

Vasarely, Victor. *Notes Brutes*. Venice, Alfieri, 1970.

Wong, Wucius. *Principles of Three-Dimensional Design*. New York: Van Nostrand Reinhold, 1977.

Materials and Processes

Wood

Brodatz, Philip. *Wood and Wood Grains: A Photographic Album for Artists and Designers*. New York: Dover, 1972.

Constantine, Albert. *Know Your Woods*. New York: Charles Scribner, 1972.

English, Kevin. *Creative Approach to Basic Woodwork*. San Francisco: Cowman, 1969.

Fendelman, Helaine. *Tramp Art: An Itinerant's Folk Art*. New York: E. P. Dutton, 1975.

Forgione, Joseph, and Sterling McIlhany. *Wood Inlay*. New York: Van Nostrand Reinhold, 1973.

Hayward, Charles H. *Complete Book of Woodwork*. New York: Drake, 1972.

Joyce, Ernest. *The Encyclopedia of Furniture Making*. New York: Drake, 1971.

Piepenburg, Robert. *Designs in Wood*. New York: Bruce, 1969.

Willcox, Donald. *New Design in Wood*. New York: Van Nostrand Reinhold, 1970.

Metal

Almeida, Oscar. *Metalworking*. New York: Drake, 1971.

Carron, Shirley. *Modern Pewter: Design and Technique*. New York: Van Nostrand Reinhold, 1973.

Clarke, Carl D. *Metal Casting of Sculpture and Ornament*. Butler, Maryland: Standard Arts, 1980.

D'Allemagne, Henry R. *Decorative Antique Ironwork*. New York: Dover Publications, 1968.

Forms in Metal: 275 Years of Metalsmithing in America. New York: American Crafts Council, 1975.

Glass, Fred J. *Metal Craft*. Felton, Calif.: Paragraph Press, 1971.

Hover, Otto. *Wrought Iron*. New York, Universe Books, 1969.

Metal: A Bibliography. New York: American Crafts Council, 1977.

Morton, Philip. *Contemporary Jewelry*. 2nd ed. New York: Holt, Rinehart and Winston, 1976.

Silvercraft. Elmsford, N.Y.: British Book Center, 1977.

Southwork, Susan and Michael. *Ornamental Ironwork*. Boston: David Godine, 1978.

Stone

Evans, Joan. *Pattern: A Study of Ornament in Western Europe*. 2 vols. New York: Da Capo Press, 1976.

Murphy, Seamus. *Stone Mad: A Sculptor's Life and Craft*. Boston: Routledge and Kegan, 1976.

Clay

Atil, Esin. *Ceramics from the World of Islam*. Baltimore, Garamond/Pridemark Press, 1973.

Barry, John. *American Indian Pottery*. Florence, Alabama: Books Americana, 1981.

Berenson, Paulus. *Finding One's Way with Clay*. New York: Simon and Schuster, 1972.

Bunzel, Ruth. *The Pueblo Potter.* New York: Dover Publications, 1972.

Cooper, Emmanuel. *A History of World Pottery.* New York: Larousse, 1981.

De Jonge, C. H. *Delft Ceramics.* New York: Praeger, 1970.

Espejel, Carlos. *Mexican Folk Ceramics.* Barcelona: Editorial Blume, 1975.

Fujioka, Ryoichi. *Shino and Oribe Ceramics.* New York: Kodansha International and Shibundo, 1977.

Leach, Bernard. *A Potter's Book.* Levittown, N.Y.: Transatlantic Arts, 1965.

Medley, Margaret. *The Chinese Potter.* New York: Charles Scribner, 1976.

Miserez-Schira, Georges. *The Art of Painting on Porcelain.* Radnor, Pa.: Chilton, 1974.

Nelson, Glenn. *Ceramics.* 4th ed. New York: Holt, Rinehart and Winston, 1978.

Paak, Carl E. *The Decorative Touch.* Englewood Cliffs, N.J.: Prentice-Hall, 1981.

Rhodes, Daniel. *Clay and Glazes for the Potter.* Rev. ed. Philadelphia: Chilton, 1973.

Riegger, Hal. *Raku: Art and Technique.* New York: Van Nostrand Reinhold, 1970.

Shafer, Thomas. *Pottery Decoration.* New York: Watson-Guptill, 1976.

Wildenhain, Marguerite. *Pottery: Form and Expression.* New York: Reinhold, 1962.

Yoshida, Mitsukuni. *In Search of Persian Pottery.* New York: Weatherhill, 1972.

Glass

Bernstein, Jack. *Stained Glass Craft.* New York: Macmillan, 1973.

Bovini, Giuseppe. *Ravenna Mosaics.* Greenwich, Conn.: New York Graphic, 1968.

Chagall, Marc. *The Jerusalem Windows.* New York: Braziller, 1967.

Gardner, Paul V., and James S. Plant. *Steuben: Seventy Years of American Glassblowing.* New York: Praeger, 1975.

Hutton, Helen. *Mosaic Making Techniques.* New York: Charles Scribner, 1977.

Johnson, James Rosser. *The Radiance of Chartres.* New York: Random House, 1965.

Metcalf, Robert, and Gertrude Metcalf. *Making Stained Glass.* New York: McGraw-Hill, 1972.

Tiffany. Intro. by Victor Arwas. New York: Rizzoli International, 1979.

Fiber

Albers, Anni. *On Weaving.* Middletown, Conn.: Wesleyan University Press, 1965.

Amir, Ziva. *Arabesque.* New York: Van Nostrand Reinhold, 1977.

Bath, Virginia. *Needlework in America.* New York: Viking Press, 1979.

Beagle, Peter. *American Denim.* New York: Harry Abrams, 1975.

Bishop, Robert, and Elizabeth Safanda. *A Gallery of Amish Quilts.* New York: E. P. Dutton, 1976.

Bress, Helen. *The Weaving Book.* New York: Charles Scribner, 1981.

Brown, Rachel. *The Weaving, Spinning and Dyeing Book.* New York: Alfred A. Knopf, 1978.

Bunting, Ethel-Jane W. *Shindi Tombs and Textiles: The Persistence of Pattern.* Albuquerque: The Maxwell Museum of Anthropology and the University of New Mexico Press, 1980.

Constantine, Mildred, and Jack Lenor Larsen. *Beyond Craft: The Art Fabric.* New York: Van Nostrand Reinhold, 1972.

D'Harcourt, Raoul. *Textiles of Ancient Peru and Their Techniques.* Seattle: University of Washington Press, 1974.

Elson, Vickie G. *Dowries from Kutch.* Los Angeles: Museum of Cultural History, 1979.

Gittinger, Mattiebelle. *Splendid Symbols: Textiles and Tradition in Indonesia.* Washington, D.C.: The Textile Museum, 1979.

Gostelow, Mary. *A World of Embroidery.* New York, Charles Scribner, 1975.

Held, Shirley E. *Weaving: A Handbook of the Fiber Arts.* 2nd ed. New York: Holt, Rinehart and Winston, 1978.

Holstein, Jonathan. *The Pieced Quilt.* Boston: The New York Graphic Society, 1973.

Kahlenberg, Mary Hunt, and Anthony Berlant. *The Navajo Blanket.* New York: Praeger, 1972.

Kahlenberg, Mary Hunt. *Textile Traditions of Indonesia.* Los Angeles: Los Angeles County Museum of Art, 1977.

Klimova, Nina T. *Folk Embroidery from the U.S.S.R.* New York: Van Nostrand Reinhold, 1981.

Kmit, Ann, Johanna and Loretta Luciow. *Ukranian Embroidery.* New York: Van Nostrand Reinhold, 1978.

Krevitsky, Nik. *Batik: Art and Craft.* New York: Van Nostrand Reinhold, 1973.

Larsen, Jack L., and Alfred Buhler. *The Dyer's Art.* New York: Van Nostrand Reinhold, 1977.

———— *Stitchery: Art and Craft.* New York: Van Nostrand Reinhold, 1973.

Ley, Sandra. *Russian and Other Slavic Embroidery Designs.* New York: Charles Scribner, 1976.

Mackie, Louise W., and John Thompson. *Turkmen: Tribal Carpets and Traditions.* Washington, D.C.: The Textile Museum, 1980.

Petrakis, Joan. *The Needle Arts of Greece.* New York: Charles Scribner, 1977.

Pfannschmidt, Ernest Erik. *Twentieth Century Lace.* New York: Charles Scribner, 1975.

Picton, John, and John Mack. *African Textiles.* London: The British Museum Publications, 1979.

Ramazanoglu, Gulseren. *Turkish Embroidery.* New York: Van Nostrand Reinhold, 1976.

Rossbach, Ed. *The Art of Paisley.* New York: Van Nostrand Reinhold, 1980.

Rowe, Ann Pollard. *A Century of Change in Guatemalan Textiles.* New York: Center for Inter-American Relations, 1981.

Thorpe, Azalea S., and Jack Lenor Larsen. *Elements of Weaving.* Garden City, N.Y.: Doubleday, 1978.

Wasserman, Tamara E., and Jonathan Hill. *Bolivian Indian Textiles: Traditional Designs and Costumes.* New York: Dover Publications, 1981.

Westphal, Katherine. *Dragons and Other Creatures: Chinese Embroidery.* Berkeley: Lancaster-Miller Publishers, 1979.

Yugoslavian/Croatian Folk Embroidery. New York: Van Nostrand Reinhold, 1976.

Plastics

Hollander, Harry. *Plastics for Jewelry.* New York: Watson-Guptill, 1974.

Newman, Jay, and Lee Newman. *Plastics for the Craftsman.* New York: Crown, 1973.

Newman, Thelma. *Plastics as Design Form.* Philadelphia: Chilton, 1972.

Plastic as Plastic. New York: Museum of Contemporary Crafts, 1969.

Quarmby, Arthur. *Plastics and Architecture.* New York: Praeger, 1974.

Rees, David. *Creative Plastics.* New York: Viking, 1973.

Painting

Gardner's *Art Through the Ages*. 7th ed. Rev. by Horst de la Croix and Richard G. Tansey. New York: Harcourt, Brace, Jovanovich, 1980.

Gaunt, William. *The Impressionists*. New York: Weathervane Books, 1975.

Janson, H. W. *History of Art*. 2nd ed. Englewood Cliffs, N.J.: Prentice-Hall, 1977.

Mendelowitz, Daniel M. *A History of American Art*. 2nd ed. New York: Holt, Rinehart and Winston, 1973.

Myers, Bernard S. *The German Expressionists: A Generation in Revolt*. New York: Praeger, 1957.

Muller, Joseph-Emile. *Fauvism*. Trans. by S. E. Jones. New York: Praeger, 1967.

Parola, René. *Optical Art: Theory and Practice*. New York: Van Nostrand Reinhold, 1969.

Rosenblum, Robert. *Cubism and Twentieth-Century Art*. New York: Abrams, 1966.

Sculpture

Barbara Hepworth. London: The Tate Gallery, 1968.

Brommer, Frank. *Sculptures of the Parthenon: Metopes, Frieza, Pediments, Cult Statue*. New York: Thames Hudson, 1979.

Irving, Donald J. *Sculpture: Material and Process*. New York: Van Nostrand Reinhold, 1970.

Kelly, J. J. *The Sculptural Idea*. Minneapolis: Burgess, 1970.

Kidson, Peter. *Sculpture at Chartres*. New York: St. Martin's, 1975.

Kowal, Dennis, Jr., and Dona Z. Meilach. *Sculpture Casting*. New York: Crown, 1972.

Krauss, Rosalind. *Sculpture of David Smith: A Catalogue Raisonné*. New York: Garland, 1977.

Legg, Alicia, ed. *Sculpture of Matisse*. New York: Museum of Modern Art, 1972.

Moore, Henry. *Sculpture and Drawings 1964–73*. New York: Wittenborn, 1977.

Richter, Gisela M., ed. *Sculpture and Sculptors of the Greeks*. 4th ed. rev. and enl. New Haven: Yale University Press, 1971.

Roukes, Nicholas. *Sculpture in Plastics*. New York: Watson-Guptill, 1978.

Stone, Anna. *Sculpture: New Ideas and Techniques*. Levittown, N.Y.: Transatlantic, 1977.

Wittkower, Rudolf. *Sculpture: Processes and Principles*. New York: Harper and Row, 1977.

Wood, Jack C. *Sculpture in Wood*. New York: Da Capo, 1977.

Printmaking

Artist's Proof: The Annual of Prints and Printmaking. New York: Pratt Graphics Center and Barre Publishers. Annually.

Eichenberg, Fritz. *The Art of the Print*. New York: Abrams, 1976.

Escher, M. C. *The Graphic Works of M. C. Escher*. New York: Ballantine, 1971.

Mayor, A. Hyatt. *Prints and People*. New York: The Metropolitan Museum of Art (dist. New York Graphic), 1971.

Peterdi, Gabor. *Printmaking*. New York: Macmillan, 1971.

Robertson, Ronald G. *Contemporary Printmaking in Japan*. New York: Crown, 1965.

Ross, John, and Clare Romano. *The Complete Printmaker*. New York: The Free Press, 1972.

Saff, Donald, and Deli Sacilotto. *Printmaking: History and Process*. New York: Holt, Rinehart and Winston, 1978.

——— *Screenprinting: History and Process*. New York: Holt, Rinehart and Winston, 1979.

Graphic Design

Clarke, Beverly. *Graphic Design in Educational Television*. New York: Watson-Guptill, 1974.

Croy, Peter. *Graphic Design and Reproduction Techniques*. Rev. ed. New York: Focal Press, 1972.

Douglass, Ralph. *Calligraphic Lettering*. 3rd ed. New York: Watson-Guptill, 1975.

Ehmcke, R. H. *Graphic Trade Symbols by German Designers*. Magnolia, Mass.: Peter Smith, n.d.

52nd Annual of Advertising Editorial and Television Art and Design with the 13th Annual Copy Awards. New York: Watson-Guptill, 1973.

Graphic Design International. Philadelphia: Hastings, 1977.

Jeffares, Katherine. *Calligraphy: The Art of Beautiful Writing*. No. Hollywood, Calif.: Wilshire, 1978.

Lam, C. M., ed. *Calligrapher's Handbook*. New York: Taplinger, 1976.

Phillips, Dave. *Graphic and Optical Art Mazes*. New York: Dover, 1976.

Photography

Adams, Ansel. *Ansel Adams: Images 1923–1974*. Greenwich, Conn.: New York Graphic, 1974.

Caponigro, Paul. *Paul Caponigro*. Millerton, N.Y.: Aperture, 1972.

Cartier-Bresson, Henri. *The World of Henri Cartier-Bresson*. New York: Viking, 1968.

Dixon, Dwight R., and Paul B. Dixon. *Photography: Experiments and Projects*. New York: Macmillan, 1976.

Eisenstadt, Alfred. *Witness to Nature*. New York: Viking, 1971.

Haas, Ernst. *The Creation*. New York: Penguin, 1978.

Life Library of Photography. New York: Time-Life Books, 1970–1971.

Swedlund, Charles. *Photography*. 2nd ed. New York: Holt, Rinehart and Winston, 1981.

Varney, Vivian. *Photographer as Designer*. Worcester, Mass.: Davis Mass, 1977.

The Performing Arts

Allensworth, Carl, with Dorothy Allensworth and Clayton Rawson. *The Complete Play Production Handbook*. New York: Harper and Row, 1982.

Bay, Howard. *Stage Design*. New York: Drama Book Specialists, 1974.

Burris-Meyer, Harold, and Edward C. Cole. *Scenery for the Theater*. 3rd ed. Boston: Little, Brown, 1972.

Parker, W. Oren, and Karvey K. Smith. *Scene Design and Stage Lighting*. 4th ed. New York: Holt, Rinehart and Winston, 1979.

Pecktal, Lynn. *Designing and Painting for the Theatre*. New York: Holt, Rinehart and Winston, 1975.

Russell, Douglas. *Stage Costume Design: Theory, Technique, and Style*. New York: Appleton-Century-Crofts, 1973.

Schubert, Hannelore. *The Modern Theatre: Architecture, Stage Design, Lighting*. New York: Praeger, 1971.

Apparel

Greenwood, Kathryn M., and Mary F. Murphy. *Fashion Innovation and Mar-*

keting. New York: Macmillan, 1978.

Hamburger, Estelle. *Fashion Business: It's All Yours*. New York: Harper and Row, 1976.

Kohler, Carl. *History of Costume*. Magnolia, Mass.: Peter Smith, n.d.

Mathisen, Marilyn. *Apparel and Accessories*. New York: McGraw-Hill, 1979.

Peltz, Leslie Ruth. *Fashion Color, Line, and Design*. Indianapolis: Bobbs-Merrill, 1971.

Salomon, Rosalie K. *Fashion Design for Moderns*. New York: Fairchild, 1976.

Sproles, George B. *Fashion: Consumer Behavior Toward Dress*. Minneapolis: Burgess, 1979.

Industrial Design

Ambasz, Emilio, ed. *Italy: The New Domestic Landscape*. New York: The Museum of Modern Art, 1972.

Carrington, Noel. *Industrial Design in Britain*. Winchester, Mass.: Allen Unwin, 1976.

Drexler, Arthur. *Design Collection: Selected Objects*. New York: Museum of Modern Art, 1970.

Itten, Johannes. *Design and Form: The Basic Course at the Bauhaus*. 2nd rev. ed. New York: Van Nostrand Reinhold, 1975.

Loewy, Raymond. *Industrial Design*. New York: Overlook Press, 1980.

Portable World. New York: Museum of Contemporary Crafts, 1973.

Interiors

Ball, Victoria Kloss. *Opportunities in Interior Design*. Skokie, Ill.: National Textbook, 1977.

Faulkner, Sarah. *Planning a Home*. New York: Holt, Rinehart and Winston, 1979.

Faulkner, Ray, and Sarah Faulkner. *Inside Today's Home*. 4th ed. New York: Holt, Rinehart and Winston, 1975.

Floethe, Louise L. *Houses Around the World*. New York: Charles Scribner, 1973.

Harling, Robert, ed. *Dictionary of Design and Decoration*. New York: Viking, 1973.

Hatje, Gerd, and Peter Kaspar. *1601 Decorating Ideas for Modern Living*. New York: Abrams, 1974.

Larsen, Jack L., and Jeanne Weeks. *Fabrics for Interiors*. New York: Van Nostrand Reinhold, 1975.

Magnani, Franco, ed. *Living Spaces: 150 Design Ideas from Around the World*. New York: Whitney Library of Design, 1978.

Philip, Peter. *Furniture of the World*. New York: Mayflower, 1978.

Phillips, Derek. *Planning Your Lighting*. New York: Quick Fox, 1978.

Stoddard, Alexandra. *Style for Living*. Garden City: Doubleday, 1974.

Zakas, Spiros. *Lifespace and Designs for Today's Living*. New York: Macmillan, 1977.

Architecture

Bloomer, Kent C., and Charles W. Moore. *Body, Memory and Architecture*. New Haven: Yale University Press, 1977.

Boericke, Art, and Barry Shapiro. *Handmade Houses: A Guide to the Woodbutcher's Art*. San Francisco: Scrimshaw, 1973.

Giedion, Siegfried. *Architecture and the Phenomena of Transition: The Three Space Conceptions in Architecture*. Cambridge, Mass.: Harvard University Press, 1971.

Gombrich, E. H. *The Sense of Order*. Oxford: Phaidon, 1979.

Gropius, Walter. *The New Architecture and the Bauhaus*. Cambridge, Mass.: MIT Press, 1968.

Hoyt, Charles King. *More Places for People*. New York: McGraw-Hill, 1982.

Jencks, Charles. *The Language of Post-Modern Architecture*. New York: Rizzoli, 1977.

Johnson, Timothy E. *Solar Architecture: The Direct Gain Approach*. New York: McGraw-Hill, 1982.

Moholy-Nagy, Sibyl. *Native Genius in Anonymous Architecture in North America*. New York: Schocken, 1976.

The Total Environment

Bacon, Edmund N. *Design of Cities*. New York: Penguin, 1976.

Bring, Mitchell, and Josse Wayembergh. *Japanese Gardens: Design and Meaning*. New York: McGraw-Hill, 1982.

Diekelmann, John, and Robert Schuster. *Natural Landscaping*. New York: McGraw-Hill, 1982.

Eckbo, Garrett. *Home Landscape: The Art of Home Landscaping*, rev. and enl. ed. New York: McGraw-Hill, 1982.

Gruen, Victor, and Larry Smith. *Centers for Urban Environment*. New York: Van Nostrand Reinhold, 1973.

Kepes, Gyorgy, ed. *Arts of the Environment*. New York: Braziller, 1972.

Kurtz, Stephen A. *Wasteland: Building the American Dream*. New York: Praeger, 1973.

Le Corbusier. *Towards a New Architecture*. New York: Praeger, 1970.

Lynch, Kevin. *Managing the Sense of a Region*. Cambridge, Mass.: MIT Press, 1976.

Mumford, Lewis. *Culture of Cities*. New York: Harcourt, Brace, Jovanovich, 1970.

——— *Roots of Contemporary American Architecture*. New York: Dover, 1972.

Index

Photographic credits

The author and publisher wish to thank the custodians of the works of art for supplying photographs and granting permission to use them. Photographs have been obtained from sources listed in the captions, unless listed below.

A/AR: Alinari/Art Resource, New York
AMNH: American Museum of Natural History, New York
BN: Bibliothèque Nationale, Paris
G/AR: Giraudon, Paris/Art Resource
H: Hirmer, Munich
HB: Hedrich Blessing, Chicago
HRV: H. Roger Violett, Paris
M: Marburg, Marburg/Lahn
NYPL: New York Public Library
NmcG: Norman McGrath, New York
PM: Philip Molten, Tiburon, California
PR: Photo Researchers, New York
RS: From Crafts of the Modern World, by Rose Slivka with the World Arts Council, and Horizon Press, © Rose Slivka.
S/AR: Scala/Art Resource, New York
WS: Willard Stone

References are to boldface figure numbers.

Color Plates:
Plate 3: Eric Pollitzer, Plate 4: Ampliaciones y Reproduciones, Barcelona. Plate 6: G/AR. Plate 7: The Vasarely Center, New York. Plates 17 and 18: Phaidon Press Ltd., Oxford, The Bridgeman Art Library, London. Plate 20: Service de Documentation Photographie de la Réunion des Musées Nationaux, Paris. Plate 21: Lester Kierstead Henderson, Cover Illustration of The Sublime Heritage of Martha Mood, Volume II, Published 1983 by Kierstead Publications, Monterey. Plate 22: Evelyn Hofer, New York. Cleve Gray.

Chapter 1   2: AMNH. 5: A/AR. 6: Grant M. Haist/National Audubon Society, PR. 8: Fotocielo, Rome. 11: Bulloz, Paris. 13: A/AR. 14: Photograph by David Smith at his home. 17: Docutel/Olivetti Corporation, New York. 18: Canadian Government Office of Tourism, Ottawa. 20: AMNH. 21: Dr. Howard E. Bigelow, University of Massachusetts, Amherst.

Chapter 2   26: Gladys Walker, Seattle. 27: Hoffritz International, Hammond/Keehn, Inc., New York. 29: Geary's, Beverly Hills. 32: Malcolm Grear Designers, Inc., Providence. 33: Walt Quade, Eastsound, Washington. 36: Markline Company, Waltham, Massachusetts. 37: Robert Walsh, New York. 39: AMNH. 42: Ken Karp, New York. 43: General Electric Company, Bridgeport. 44: US Suzuki Motor Corporation, Brea, California.

Chapter 3   45: Shigeo Anzai, Tokyo. 47: NYPL. 49: From Forms and Patterns in Nature, by Wolf Strache, Random House, New York. 50: Charles Moore, Black Star, New York. 52: Asian Art Photographic Distribution, New York. 53: Walt Quade, Eastsound, Washington, From Chinese Written Characters: Their Wit and Wisdom, by Rose Quong, Cobble Hill Press, 1968, New York. 59: Roger Marschutz, Los Angeles. 60: Massachusetts Institute of Technology.

Chapter 4   71: The British Tourist Authority, New York. 72: AMNH. 74: Antonia Graeber, Los Angeles. 75: Leo Castelli Gallery, New York. 76: George Jennings, Jr., Norwich, Conn. 77: RS. 78: Tung Yah Asian Arts, La Jolla, California. 82: Jan Lukas, PR. 88: Helmsley Spear, Inc., New York. 90: Nat Norman, PR. 91: Roger Werth for Longview Daily News, 1980, Woodfin Camp, New York. 96: M. Lee Fatherree. 97: Russell Dixon Lamb/PR.

Chapter 5   103 and 104: WS. 112: Magnum, New York. 113: Julius Shulman, LA. 114: AMNH. 115: Caisse Nationale des Monuments Historiques et des Sites, Paris. 118: Kissarvik Cooperative, Rankin, N.W.T. Canada. 120 and 121: A/AR. 124: Harry Murphy + Friends, Mill Valley.

Chapter 6   128: ARCO Center for Visual Art, LA. 135 and 136: © NM. 139 and 140: RS. 141: Asian Art Photographic Distribution, New York. 143: H. 144: From The New Churches of Europe, by G. E. Kidder Smith. 146 and 147: Antonia Graeber, LA. 152: RS.
Chapter 7   155: From Munsell: A Grammar of Color copyright © 1969 by Reinhold Publishing. Reprinted by permission of Van Nostrand Reinhold Company, New York. 159: LWT International, London. 160: AMNH.
Chapter 8   163: AMNH. 167: © 1982 Trustees of Princeton University. 171: Anne Odom, Washington, D.C.
Chapter 9   172: Myron Wood, PR. 175: Henri Cartier-Bresson, Magnum. 178: S/AR. 183: Nathan Rabin, New York. 189: RS.
Chapter 10   191: Allen Mewbourne, Houston. 192: The Bettmann Archive, Inc., New York. 194: Alison Frantz, Princeton, New Jersey. 198: Eastman Kodak Company, Rochester, New York. 200: A/AR. 201: AMNH. 203: Robert d'Estrube, Stephen Lowe Art Gallery, Victoria, B.C. 207: Wilhelm Rauh, The Bayreuth Festival, Bayreuth, West Germany.

Works by Mondrian, Escher: © Beeldrecht, Amsterdam/VAGA, New York, 1984. Rodin, Picasso, Matisse, Leger, Vasarely, Le Corbusier, Ensor, Renoir: © SPADEM, Paris/VAGA, New York. David Smith: © Estate of David Smith, 1984. Romano: © Clare Romano; Courtesy Association of American Artists, 1984. Remington: © Deborah Remington, 1983. Rauschenberg: © Robert Rauschenberg, 1984. Westermann: © Estate of H.C. Westermann. de Chirico: S.I.A.E., Italy/VAGA, New York, 1984. Warhol: © Andy Warhol, 1984. Rosenquist: © James Rosenquist. Anuszkiewicz: © Richard Anuszkiewicz. Miro, Giacometti, Dubuffet, Calder, Gleizes, Magritte, Chagall, Duchamp, Kandinsky, Brancusi, Arp, Cassatt: © ADAGP, 1984.